50 Japan Winter Season Recipes for Home

By: Kelly Johnson

Table of Contents

- Nabe (Japanese Hot Pot)
- Oden (Japanese Winter Stew)
- Kiritanpo (Grilled Rice Sticks)
- Sukiyaki
- Shabu-Shabu
- Miso Soup with Tofu and Wakame
- Tempura Udon
- Yudofu (Hot Pot Tofu)
- Kabocha Squash Soup
- Chanko Nabe (Sumo Stew)
- Oyakodon (Chicken and Egg Rice Bowl)
- Nikujaga (Japanese Meat and Potato Stew)
- Zoni (New Year's Mochi Soup)
- Tori Kotsu Ramen (Chicken Bone Ramen)
- Karaage (Japanese Fried Chicken)
- Tamagoyaki (Japanese Omelette)
- Miso Katsu (Miso-Glazed Pork Cutlet)
- Yakiniku (Grilled Meat)
- Takikomi Gohan (Mixed Rice)
- Chashu Pork (Braised Pork Belly)
- Okonomiyaki (Savory Pancake)
- Kakuni (Braised Pork Belly)
- Korokke (Croquettes)
- Katsudon (Pork Cutlet Rice Bowl)
- Goya Champuru (Bitter Melon Stir-Fry)
- Soba Noodle Soup
- Butajiru (Pork and Vegetable Miso Soup)
- Kuri Gohan (Chestnut Rice)
- Kiritanpo Nabe (Rice Stick Hot Pot)
- Satsuma Age (Deep-Fried Fish Cake)
- Yudofu (Tofu Hot Pot)
- Buta Kakuni (Braised Pork Belly)

- Niku Miso (Meat Miso)
- Shoyu Ramen (Soy Sauce Ramen)
- Oden (Winter Stew)
- Miso Ramen
- Miso Soup with Mushrooms
- Kabocha Tempura (Pumpkin Tempura)
- Katsudon (Pork Cutlet Rice Bowl)
- Tori Dango (Chicken Meatballs)
- Shio Ramen (Salt Ramen)
- Nabeyaki Udon (Hot Pot Udon)
- Kakiage (Mixed Vegetable Tempura)
- Miso Yaki Onigiri (Grilled Rice Balls)
- Tori Kotsu Ramen (Chicken Bone Broth Ramen)
- Kimchi Nabe (Kimchi Hot Pot)
- Udon in Broth
- Mochi Soup with Vegetables
- Mizutaki (Chicken Hot Pot)
- Miso-Glazed Eggplant

Nabe (Japanese Hot Pot)

Ingredients:

For the Broth:

- **4 cups dashi stock** (homemade or from a dashi packet)
- **1/4 cup soy sauce**
- **2 tablespoons mirin**
- **2 tablespoons sake**
- **1 tablespoon sugar** (optional, to taste)

For the Hot Pot:

- **200g (7 oz) thinly sliced beef** (or pork, chicken, or seafood)
- **200g (7 oz) tofu**, cut into cubes
- **2 cups napa cabbage**, chopped
- **1 cup shiitake mushrooms**, sliced
- **1 cup enoki mushrooms**, trimmed
- **1 cup bok choy**, chopped
- **1 large carrot**, sliced thinly
- **1-2 scallions**, chopped
- **1-2 cups udon noodles** or **soba noodles** (optional)
- **1 cup daikon radish**, sliced (optional)
- **1/2 cup fresh spinach** (optional)
- **1/2 cup Chinese cabbage** (optional)
- **1 cup sliced onions** (optional)

For Serving:

- **Cooked rice** (optional)
- **Chopsticks** or **tongs** (for serving)
- **Dipping sauces** like ponzu or sesame sauce (optional)

Instructions:

1. Prepare the Broth:

- **Combine Ingredients:** In a large pot, combine the dashi stock, soy sauce, mirin, sake, and sugar (if using).
- **Simmer:** Bring the mixture to a gentle simmer over medium heat. Taste and adjust seasoning if needed.

2. Prepare the Ingredients:

- **Slice Vegetables and Proteins:** Cut the beef or other proteins into bite-sized pieces. Slice the vegetables and mushrooms as needed.
- **Arrange Ingredients:** Arrange all the ingredients on a large platter or tray for easy access.

3. **Cook the Nabe:**

- **Heat Pot:** Bring the broth to a simmer in the pot.
- **Add Ingredients:** Start by adding the harder vegetables like carrots and daikon radish. Simmer until they begin to soften, about 5-10 minutes.
- **Add Proteins:** Add the sliced beef, tofu, and any other proteins. Cook until the meat is just done. If using seafood, add it last as it cooks quickly.
- **Add Noodles:** If using noodles, add them towards the end of the cooking time so they don't become overcooked.

4. **Serve the Nabe:**

- **Serve Hot:** Transfer the pot to the table and let everyone help themselves. Use chopsticks or tongs to pick out cooked ingredients from the pot.
- **Enjoy with Rice:** You can also serve the nabe with a side of cooked rice to soak up the delicious broth.
- **Dipping Sauces:** Offer dipping sauces like ponzu or sesame sauce for additional flavor.

Tips:

- **Customization:** Feel free to customize your nabe with seasonal vegetables, different types of mushrooms, or other proteins like shrimp, fish, or sausages.
- **Broth Variations:** Experiment with different types of broths such as miso-based or shoyu-based, depending on your preference.
- **One-Pot Cooking:** Nabe is a great way to use up leftover vegetables and meats. Just ensure that all ingredients are cut into similar sizes for even cooking.
- **Keep it Simmering:** If you're eating over a longer period, keep the pot at a low simmer to ensure the broth stays hot and ingredients remain tender.

Nabe is not just a meal but a social experience, bringing warmth and togetherness to your table. Enjoy your hot pot!

Oden (Japanese Winter Stew)

Ingredients:

For the Broth:

- **4 cups dashi stock** (homemade or from a dashi packet)
- **1/4 cup soy sauce**
- **1/4 cup mirin**
- **2 tablespoons sake**
- **2 tablespoons sugar** (adjust to taste)

For the Stew:

- **1 block of tofu**, cut into cubes (or tofu puffs if available)
- **1 daikon radish**, peeled and sliced into rounds
- **4-6 pieces of konnyaku** (konjac), cut into triangles or slices
- **4-6 fish cakes** (various types like chikuwa or satsuma-age)
- **2-4 boiled eggs**
- **2-3 types of mushrooms** (shiitake, shimeji, or enoki), cleaned and trimmed
- **1 cup of small potatoes**, peeled (optional)
- **1-2 pieces of taro root**, peeled and cut into chunks (optional)
- **1-2 pieces of kamaboko** (steamed fish cake), sliced (optional)
- **1-2 pieces of mochi** (Japanese rice cakes), optional but delicious

For Garnish (optional):

- **Chopped scallions**
- **Shichimi togarashi** (seven-spice blend) or **karashi** (Japanese mustard)

Instructions:

1. Prepare the Broth:

- **Combine Ingredients:** In a large pot, combine the dashi stock, soy sauce, mirin, sake, and sugar.
- **Simmer:** Bring the mixture to a gentle simmer over medium heat. Taste and adjust the seasoning if needed.

2. Prepare the Ingredients:

- **Daikon:** Slice the daikon radish into rounds and lightly score the surface with a knife to allow the flavor to penetrate.
- **Konnyaku:** Cut the konnyaku into triangles or slices. Blanch in boiling water for a few minutes to remove its distinctive smell, then drain.
- **Fish Cakes:** Slice or cut the fish cakes into bite-sized pieces if needed.

- **Boiled Eggs:** If not already done, boil the eggs for about 8-10 minutes, then peel them.
- **Potatoes and Taro:** Peel and cut the potatoes and taro root into chunks. Parboil them for about 5 minutes to partially cook before adding to the stew.

3. Cook the Oden:

- **Simmer Ingredients:** Add the prepared ingredients to the simmering broth, starting with the hardest items like daikon, potatoes, and taro.
- **Add Fish Cakes and Tofu:** After 10-15 minutes, add the fish cakes, tofu, and mushrooms.
- **Simmer Gently:** Let the stew simmer gently for 30-40 minutes, or until all the ingredients are tender and have absorbed the flavors of the broth.

4. Serve the Oden:

- **Serve Hot:** Ladle the oden into bowls, making sure to include a variety of ingredients in each serving.
- **Garnish:** Garnish with chopped scallions, shichimi togarashi, or a dollop of karashi if desired.

Tips:

- **Ingredient Variations:** Oden is very adaptable. Feel free to add other ingredients like lotus root, bamboo shoots, or different types of fish cakes based on your preference.
- **Flavor Development:** Oden often tastes even better the next day as the flavors continue to meld. It's a great dish for making ahead.
- **Broth Adjustments:** Adjust the sweetness and saltiness of the broth to your taste. Some people prefer a slightly sweeter or saltier broth.

Oden is not only a warming and satisfying meal but also a great way to enjoy a variety of ingredients in a single pot. It's perfect for sharing with family and friends on a cold day. Enjoy your cozy and flavorful Japanese stew!

Kiritanpo (Grilled Rice Sticks)

Ingredients:

- **2 cups short-grain or sushi rice**
- **2 1/2 cups water**
- **1/4 teaspoon salt**
- **Bamboo skewers** (soaked in water for 30 minutes to prevent burning)

For Serving (optional):

- **Miso sauce** (recipe below)
- **Soy sauce**
- **Pickled vegetables**

Instructions:

1. Prepare the Rice:

- **Wash Rice:** Rinse the rice under cold water until the water runs clear. This helps to remove excess starch.
- **Cook Rice:** In a rice cooker or a pot, combine the rice and water. Cook according to the manufacturer's instructions or bring to a boil, then reduce to a simmer, cover, and cook for about 18-20 minutes until the water is absorbed and the rice is tender. Let it sit for 10 minutes, then fluff with a fork.

2. Shape the Rice Sticks:

- **Prepare Skewers:** While the rice is still warm, take a handful of rice and mold it around a bamboo skewer, forming a cylinder about 1/2 inch thick and 3-4 inches long. Press the rice firmly onto the skewer so that it stays in place.
- **Repeat:** Continue this process with the remaining rice and skewers.

3. Grill the Rice Sticks:

- **Preheat Grill or Pan:** Preheat a grill or a grill pan over medium heat. You can also use a broiler or even a regular skillet if you don't have access to a grill.
- **Grill Rice Sticks:** Place the rice sticks on the grill or in the pan. Cook for about 2-3 minutes on each side, or until they develop a golden-brown, slightly crispy exterior. Keep an eye on them to avoid burning.

4. Prepare Miso Sauce (optional):

- **Ingredients for Miso Sauce:**
    - **3 tablespoons miso paste** (white or red)
    - **2 tablespoons sugar**

- - **1 tablespoon mirin**
  - **1 tablespoon sake** (optional)
  - **1 teaspoon soy sauce**
- **Combine Ingredients:** In a small saucepan, combine the miso paste, sugar, mirin, sake, and soy sauce.
- **Cook:** Heat over medium-low heat, stirring constantly until the mixture is smooth and slightly thickened. Remove from heat and let cool.

5. Serve the Kiritanpo:

- **Serve with Sauce:** Brush or dip the grilled rice sticks in the miso sauce, or serve it on the side for dipping.
- **Enjoy with Pickles:** Kiritanpo is often enjoyed with pickled vegetables for a refreshing contrast.

Tips:

- **Rice Texture:** Make sure the rice is still warm and sticky when molding onto skewers. This helps it adhere better.
- **Grilling:** If using a grill pan or broiler, watch the rice sticks closely as they can burn quickly.
- **Miso Sauce Variations:** Adjust the sweetness and saltiness of the miso sauce according to your taste. You can also add other flavorings like garlic or ginger if desired.

Kiritanpo is a delightful and unique Japanese treat, offering a blend of chewy and crispy textures. It's perfect for a snack, appetizer, or even as a side dish in a larger meal. Enjoy making and sharing this traditional dish!

Sukiyaki

Ingredients:

For the Sukiyaki:

- **300g (10 oz) thinly sliced beef** (ribeye or sirloin)
- **1 block of tofu**, cut into cubes
- **1 cup shirataki noodles** or **udon noodles**
- **2 cups napa cabbage**, chopped
- **1 cup mushrooms** (shiitake, enoki, or oyster), sliced
- **1 large carrot**, sliced thinly
- **1 cup bamboo shoots** (canned or fresh), sliced
- **1-2 scallions**, sliced
- **1-2 eggs** (optional, for dipping)

For the Sukiyaki Sauce (Warishita):

- **1/2 cup soy sauce**
- **1/4 cup mirin**
- **1/4 cup sake**
- **2 tablespoons sugar**
- **1/4 cup dashi stock** (optional, but adds depth)

Instructions:

1. Prepare the Ingredients:

- **Beef:** Slice the beef into thin strips if not pre-sliced.
- **Tofu:** Cut the tofu into bite-sized cubes.
- **Noodles:** If using shirataki noodles, rinse and drain them. If using udon noodles, cook according to package instructions and set aside.
- **Vegetables and Mushrooms:** Slice the vegetables and mushrooms as needed.
- **Scallions:** Slice the scallions into thin rings.

2. Prepare the Sukiyaki Sauce (Warishita):

- **Combine Ingredients:** In a bowl, mix together soy sauce, mirin, sake, sugar, and dashi stock (if using). Stir until the sugar is dissolved.

3. Cook the Sukiyaki:

- **Preheat the Pot:** Heat a large, deep skillet or a sukiyaki pot over medium heat. You can also use a hot pot or an electric skillet.
- **Add Sauce:** Pour a small amount of the sukiyaki sauce into the pot and heat until it begins to simmer.

- **Add Beef:** Place the beef slices in the pot and cook briefly until they begin to brown.
- **Add Vegetables and Tofu:** Add the tofu, vegetables, mushrooms, and bamboo shoots to the pot. Pour in more of the sukiyaki sauce to cover the ingredients.
- **Simmer:** Let the ingredients simmer for about 10-15 minutes, or until the vegetables are tender and the flavors have melded together. You can adjust the seasoning with additional soy sauce or sugar if needed.
- **Add Noodles:** If using udon or shirataki noodles, add them during the last few minutes of cooking to heat through.

4. Serve the Sukiyaki:

- **At the Table:** Serve the sukiyaki hot from the pot. It's common to have a small bowl of raw egg (beaten) for dipping the cooked ingredients before eating. The egg is optional and is often used to add a creamy texture.
- **Enjoy:** Scoop out ingredients and enjoy with rice or noodles.

Tips:

- **Beef Choice:** Choose well-marbled beef for the best flavor and tenderness. If you can't find thinly sliced beef, you can freeze it for about an hour to make it easier to slice thinly.
- **Customize Ingredients:** Sukiyaki is quite versatile. Feel free to add other ingredients such as lotus root, snap peas, or different types of mushrooms based on your preferences.
- **Vegetarian Option:** For a vegetarian version, substitute the beef with mushrooms or seitan and use vegetable broth instead of dashi. Adjust the seasonings as needed.

Sukiyaki is a wonderful way to enjoy a variety of ingredients cooked together in a rich, flavorful sauce. It's perfect for sharing with family and friends, making it both a delicious and social dining experience. Enjoy your meal!

Shabu-Shabu

Ingredients:

For the Broth:

- **4 cups dashi stock** (homemade or from a dashi packet)
- **1-2 cups water** (as needed)
- **1-2 tablespoons soy sauce** (to taste)
- **1 tablespoon sake**
- **1 tablespoon mirin**

For the Hot Pot:

- **300g (10 oz) thinly sliced beef** (ribeye, sirloin, or other tender cuts)
- **1 block of tofu**, cut into cubes
- **1 cup mushrooms** (shiitake, enoki, or shimeji), cleaned and trimmed
- **2 cups napa cabbage**, chopped
- **1 large carrot**, sliced thinly
- **1 cup spinach** or **bok choy**
- **1 cup sliced onions**
- **1 cup udon noodles** or **soba noodles** (optional)
- **1 cup bean sprouts** (optional)
- **2-3 scallions**, sliced (optional)

For Dipping Sauces (optional):

- **Ponzu sauce** (citrus-soy sauce)
- **Sesame dipping sauce**
- **Chili oil** or **shichimi togarashi** (Japanese seven-spice blend) for added spice

Instructions:

1. Prepare the Broth:

- **Combine Ingredients:** In a large pot, combine the dashi stock, water, soy sauce, sake, and mirin.
- **Simmer:** Bring to a gentle simmer over medium heat. Adjust the seasoning to taste if needed. Keep the broth simmering gently throughout the meal.

2. Prepare the Ingredients:

- **Beef:** Slice the beef into thin strips if not pre-sliced. This helps it cook quickly in the hot pot.
- **Tofu:** Cut the tofu into bite-sized cubes.

- **Vegetables and Mushrooms:** Slice and prepare the vegetables and mushrooms. If using carrots, slice them thinly so they cook quickly.
- **Noodles:** If using noodles, cook according to package instructions and set aside.
- **Scallions and Bean Sprouts:** Prepare and set aside.

3. Cook the Shabu-Shabu:

- **Heat the Pot:** Place the pot with the simmering broth at the center of the table. This allows everyone to cook their own ingredients.
- **Cook Ingredients:** Using chopsticks or a slotted spoon, cook the thinly sliced beef, vegetables, tofu, and mushrooms in the simmering broth. Cook each item for a few seconds to a minute, depending on thickness and personal preference.
- **Add Noodles:** If using noodles, add them during the last few minutes of cooking to heat through.

4. Serve the Shabu-Shabu:

- **Dipping Sauces:** Provide a selection of dipping sauces such as ponzu or sesame sauce. You can also offer chili oil or shichimi togarashi for extra flavor.
- **Enjoy:** Scoop out cooked ingredients into individual bowls. Dip in the sauces and enjoy with rice or noodles.

Tips:

- **Beef Choice:** Use high-quality beef for the best flavor. Thinly sliced beef is essential for quick cooking and a tender texture.
- **Customizable:** Shabu-shabu is highly customizable. Feel free to add other ingredients like lotus root, bamboo shoots, or different types of mushrooms based on your preference.
- **Broth:** Keep the broth at a gentle simmer to avoid overcooking the ingredients. You can also replenish the broth as needed during the meal.

Shabu-Shabu is a fun and interactive way to enjoy a variety of fresh ingredients cooked quickly in a flavorful broth. It's perfect for a group meal and provides a warm, satisfying dining experience. Enjoy your hot pot!

Miso Soup with Tofu and Wakame

Ingredients:

- **4 cups dashi stock** (homemade or from a dashi packet)
- **1/4 cup miso paste** (white or red, depending on your preference)
- **1 block of tofu**, cut into small cubes
- **1/4 cup dried wakame seaweed**
- **2-3 scallions**, sliced
- **1 tablespoon soy sauce** (optional, to taste)
- **1 teaspoon sesame oil** (optional, for added flavor)

Instructions:

1. Prepare the Dashi Stock:

- **Heat Dashi:** In a medium pot, bring the dashi stock to a simmer over medium heat.

2. Rehydrate the Wakame:

- **Soak Wakame:** Place the dried wakame in a bowl of water and let it soak for about 10 minutes, or until it expands and becomes tender. Drain and cut into bite-sized pieces if needed.

3. Prepare the Tofu:

- **Cut Tofu:** While the wakame is soaking, cut the tofu into small cubes. You can use either firm or soft tofu based on your preference.

4. Add Tofu and Wakame:

- **Simmer:** Add the cubed tofu and rehydrated wakame to the simmering dashi stock. Let it heat through for about 3-5 minutes.

5. Incorporate the Miso Paste:

- **Dissolve Miso:** In a small bowl, mix the miso paste with a ladleful of hot dashi stock from the pot to dissolve it. This helps to prevent clumps of miso in the soup.
- **Add Miso to Soup:** Stir the dissolved miso paste back into the pot. Heat the soup gently but do not let it boil, as boiling can affect the flavor and texture of the miso.

6. Season and Garnish:

- **Adjust Flavor:** Taste the soup and adjust seasoning if needed. Add soy sauce if you prefer a slightly saltier flavor, and sesame oil for added depth.
- **Garnish:** Add sliced scallions as a garnish.

7. Serve:

- **Dish Up:** Ladle the miso soup into bowls and serve hot.

Tips:

- **Miso Paste:** Use white miso for a milder flavor or red miso for a more robust taste. You can also use a blend of both.
- **Avoid Boiling:** Once the miso paste is added, avoid boiling the soup to maintain its delicate flavor.
- **Variations:** You can add other ingredients like mushrooms, thinly sliced carrots, or even a few drops of sesame oil to enhance the flavor.

Miso Soup with Tofu and Wakame is a staple in Japanese cuisine, offering a healthy and comforting bowl of soup that is perfect for any meal. Enjoy the soothing and rich flavors of this classic dish!

Tempura Udon

Ingredients:

For the Udon Soup:

- **4 cups dashi stock** (homemade or from a dashi packet)
- **1/4 cup soy sauce**
- **1/4 cup mirin**
- **1 tablespoon sake** (optional)
- **1 teaspoon sugar** (optional, adjust to taste)
- **2 servings of udon noodles** (fresh or frozen, cooked according to package instructions)
- **2-3 scallions**, sliced
- **1/4 cup sliced mushrooms** (shiitake, enoki, or button mushrooms), optional
- **2-3 sheets of nori**, cut into strips (optional)

For the Tempura:

- **1/2 cup all-purpose flour**
- **1/2 cup cornstarch**
- **1/2 teaspoon baking powder**
- **1/2 teaspoon salt**
- **1 large egg**, lightly beaten
- **1 cup cold water** (adjust as needed)
- **Vegetable oil** (for frying)

Tempura Ingredients:

- **1-2 large shrimp**, peeled and deveined
- **1 small sweet potato**, peeled and sliced thinly
- **1 small zucchini**, sliced thinly
- **1 small bell pepper**, sliced thinly
- **1-2 mushrooms**, sliced (optional)

Instructions:

1. Prepare the Tempura Batter:

- **Mix Dry Ingredients:** In a bowl, combine the flour, cornstarch, baking powder, and salt.
- **Add Wet Ingredients:** In a separate bowl, lightly beat the egg and mix it with the cold water.
- **Combine:** Add the egg mixture to the dry ingredients and stir until just combined. The batter should be lumpy; don't overmix.

2. Prepare the Tempura Ingredients:

- **Heat Oil:** Heat vegetable oil in a deep pan or fryer to 350°F (175°C). There should be enough oil to submerge the tempura ingredients.
- **Coat Ingredients:** Dip the shrimp and vegetables into the tempura batter, allowing excess batter to drip off.
- **Fry Tempura:** Carefully place the battered ingredients into the hot oil. Fry until golden brown and crispy, about 2-3 minutes for shrimp and 3-4 minutes for vegetables. Remove with a slotted spoon and drain on paper towels.

3. **Prepare the Udon Soup:**

- **Make the Broth:** In a large pot, combine the dashi stock, soy sauce, mirin, sake (if using), and sugar (if using). Heat until it reaches a simmer.
- **Add Vegetables:** Add sliced mushrooms (if using) and let them cook for a few minutes until tender.
- **Add Udon Noodles:** Add the cooked udon noodles to the pot and heat through.

4. **Assemble the Dish:**

- **Serve Udon:** Divide the udon noodles between bowls.
- **Add Broth:** Ladle the hot broth and vegetables over the noodles.
- **Top with Tempura:** Place the freshly fried tempura on top of the noodles.

5. **Garnish and Serve:**

- **Garnish:** Sprinkle with sliced scallions and nori strips if desired.
- **Serve Hot:** Enjoy the tempura udon while it's hot and crispy.

Tips:

- **Tempura Oil Temperature:** Ensure the oil is at the right temperature before frying to get a crispy texture. If the oil is too hot, the tempura will burn; if it's too cold, it will be greasy.
- **Noodle Cooking:** If using dried udon noodles, follow package instructions for cooking. Fresh or frozen udon noodles may only need a quick reheating in the broth.
- **Variations:** You can add other toppings such as sliced green onions, a sprinkle of sesame seeds, or a soft-boiled egg if desired.

Tempura Udon is a satisfying dish that combines the comforting elements of a warm noodle soup with the crispiness of tempura. It's perfect for a hearty meal that's both flavorful and texturally interesting. Enjoy your cooking!

Yudofu (Hot Pot Tofu)

Ingredients:

For the Yudofu:

- **1 block of firm or silken tofu**, cut into large cubes
- **4 cups dashi stock** (homemade or from a dashi packet)
- **1-2 cups of leafy greens** (such as spinach, bok choy, or napa cabbage), chopped
- **1-2 scallions**, sliced
- **1 cup mushrooms** (shiitake, enoki, or shimeji), sliced (optional)

For Dipping Sauces (optional):

- **Ponzu sauce** (citrus-soy sauce)
- **Sesame dipping sauce**
- **Grated daikon radish** (for garnish)
- **Shichimi togarashi** (Japanese seven-spice blend) (optional, for added spice)

Instructions:

1. Prepare the Broth:

- **Heat Dashi:** In a large pot, bring the dashi stock to a gentle simmer over medium heat.

2. Prepare the Tofu:

- **Cut Tofu:** Cut the tofu into large cubes. This helps to keep the tofu from breaking apart during cooking.

3. Add Ingredients to the Pot:

- **Simmer Tofu:** Gently add the tofu cubes to the simmering dashi stock. Allow them to heat through for about 5-10 minutes.
- **Add Vegetables and Mushrooms:** Add the leafy greens and mushrooms to the pot. Simmer for an additional 2-3 minutes until the vegetables are tender and the tofu is heated through.

4. Prepare Dipping Sauces (Optional):

- **Ponzu Sauce:** Serve ponzu sauce in small bowls for dipping.
- **Sesame Sauce:** Combine tahini or sesame paste with soy sauce, a little sugar, and a splash of rice vinegar to make a simple sesame dipping sauce.
- **Grated Daikon Radish:** Grate fresh daikon radish and serve as a garnish.

5. Serve:

- **Dish Up:** Ladle the tofu, vegetables, and broth into individual bowls. Provide dipping sauces on the side.

Tips:

- **Broth Flavor:** The dashi stock provides a mild and umami-rich flavor. You can adjust the seasoning with a bit of soy sauce if you prefer a stronger taste.
- **Tofu Type:** Firm tofu is commonly used for its texture, but silken tofu can be used for a more delicate, creamy texture.
- **Vegetables:** Feel free to customize the vegetables based on what you have on hand or personal preference. Root vegetables like carrots and potatoes can also be added.

Yudofu is a versatile and soothing dish that emphasizes the natural flavors of tofu and vegetables. It's perfect for a light and warming meal, especially during colder months. Enjoy the simplicity and comfort of this traditional Japanese hot pot!

Kabocha Squash Soup

Ingredients:

- **1 medium kabocha squash** (about 2-3 pounds), peeled, seeded, and cubed
- **1 medium onion**, chopped
- **2 cloves garlic**, minced
- **2 tablespoons olive oil** or **butter**
- **4 cups vegetable broth** or **chicken broth**
- **1 cup coconut milk** or **heavy cream** (for extra creaminess)
- **Salt and pepper** to taste
- **1/2 teaspoon ground nutmeg** (optional)
- **1/2 teaspoon ground ginger** (optional)
- **1 tablespoon soy sauce** (optional, for added depth)
- **Chopped fresh parsley** or **chives** for garnish (optional)
- **Croutons** or **toasted seeds** for garnish (optional)

Instructions:

1. Prepare the Kabocha Squash:

- **Cut and Seed:** Cut the kabocha squash in half, scoop out the seeds, and discard them.
- **Peel and Cube:** Peel the squash with a vegetable peeler or knife. Cut the flesh into 1-inch cubes.

2. Cook the Aromatics:

- **Heat Oil:** In a large pot, heat the olive oil or butter over medium heat.
- **Sauté Onion and Garlic:** Add the chopped onion and cook until translucent, about 5 minutes. Add the minced garlic and cook for an additional minute until fragrant.

3. Cook the Squash:

- **Add Squash:** Add the cubed kabocha squash to the pot. Stir to combine with the onion and garlic.
- **Add Broth:** Pour in the vegetable or chicken broth. Bring to a boil, then reduce the heat and simmer for about 20-25 minutes, or until the squash is tender and can be easily pierced with a fork.

4. Blend the Soup:

- **Puree Soup:** Use an immersion blender to blend the soup in the pot until smooth. Alternatively, you can blend the soup in batches using a countertop blender. Be cautious when blending hot liquids—allow the soup to cool slightly before blending if using a regular blender.

5. Finish the Soup:

- **Add Cream:** Stir in the coconut milk or heavy cream. Heat through without boiling.
- **Season:** Season the soup with salt, pepper, ground nutmeg, and ground ginger to taste. Add soy sauce if using, for additional umami flavor.

6. Serve:

- **Garnish:** Ladle the soup into bowls. Garnish with chopped fresh parsley or chives, and add croutons or toasted seeds if desired.
- **Enjoy:** Serve hot.

Tips:

- **Peeling Kabocha:** The skin of the kabocha squash can be tough to peel. If you prefer, you can leave the skin on while cooking and then blend the soup. The skin becomes very soft and blends smoothly.
- **Texture:** For a smoother texture, strain the soup through a fine-mesh sieve after blending, though this step is optional.
- **Flavor Variations:** Consider adding a dash of curry powder or paprika for an extra flavor boost. Fresh herbs like thyme or rosemary can also enhance the soup.

Kabocha Squash Soup is a rich, velvety soup that highlights the natural sweetness of the squash. It's perfect for warming up on a chilly day and makes a wonderful starter or main course. Enjoy!

Chanko Nabe (Sumo Stew)

Ingredients:

For the Broth:

- **6 cups dashi stock** (homemade or from a dashi packet)
- **1/4 cup soy sauce**
- **1/4 cup mirin**
- **2 tablespoons sake** (optional)
- **1 tablespoon sugar** (optional, adjust to taste)
- **1-2 tablespoons miso paste** (optional, for added depth)

For the Hot Pot:

- **1 lb chicken thighs** (boneless and skinless, cut into bite-sized pieces)
- **1/2 lb beef sirloin** (sliced thinly, optional)
- **1 block firm tofu** (cut into cubes)
- **1 cup mushrooms** (shiitake, enoki, or button mushrooms), sliced
- **2-3 carrots**, peeled and sliced
- **1-2 potatoes**, peeled and cut into chunks
- **1 bunch of bok choy** (or Napa cabbage), chopped
- **1 bunch green onions**, sliced
- **1-2 cups daikon radish**, peeled and sliced
- **1 cup sliced bamboo shoots** (optional)
- **1 cup fresh or frozen udon noodles** (optional, cooked according to package instructions)
- **Chili oil** or **togarashi** (Japanese chili pepper) for serving (optional)

Instructions:

1. Prepare the Broth:

- **Combine Ingredients:** In a large pot, combine the dashi stock, soy sauce, mirin, sake (if using), and sugar. Heat over medium heat until it reaches a simmer.
- **Add Miso:** If using miso paste, dissolve it in a small amount of hot broth in a separate bowl, then stir it back into the pot. Simmer gently.

2. Prepare the Ingredients:

- **Prep Proteins:** Cut the chicken thighs into bite-sized pieces. If using beef, slice it thinly.
- **Cut Vegetables:** Prepare all vegetables and tofu, cutting them into appropriate sizes for the hot pot.

3. Cook the Hot Pot:

- **Heat Broth:** Bring the broth to a gentle simmer.
- **Add Ingredients:** Add the chicken, beef (if using), tofu, mushrooms, carrots, potatoes, daikon radish, and bamboo shoots (if using) to the pot. Simmer until the chicken is cooked through and the vegetables are tender, about 15-20 minutes.
- **Add Greens:** Add bok choy or napa cabbage and green onions, and cook for an additional 2-3 minutes until wilted.

4. Add Noodles (Optional):

- **Add Noodles:** If using udon noodles, add them to the pot and let them heat through, about 2-3 minutes.

5. Serve:

- **Dish Up:** Ladle the hot pot into bowls. Serve with additional condiments such as chili oil or togarashi if desired.
- **Enjoy:** Serve hot and enjoy!

Tips:

- **Broth Flavor:** Adjust the seasoning of the broth to your taste. Add more soy sauce for saltiness or more mirin for sweetness.
- **Variety:** Feel free to add other vegetables or ingredients according to your preference or what you have on hand, such as corn, sweet potatoes, or other types of mushrooms.
- **Cooking Time:** Ensure that the meat and vegetables are cooked through before serving. The cooking time will vary depending on the size of your cuts and the heat of your broth.

Chanko Nabe is a versatile and filling dish that brings a variety of flavors and textures to the table. It's perfect for a communal meal and can be adapted to suit your taste and dietary preferences. Enjoy this warming and satisfying stew!

Oyakodon (Chicken and Egg Rice Bowl)

Ingredients:

- **2 cups cooked Japanese short-grain rice** (or any rice you prefer)

For the Chicken and Egg Mixture:

- **1 lb (450 g) boneless, skinless chicken thighs** (or breast), cut into bite-sized pieces
- **1 small onion**, thinly sliced
- **3 large eggs**
- **1 cup dashi stock** (or chicken broth)
- **1/4 cup soy sauce**
- **1/4 cup mirin**
- **2 tablespoons sake** (optional)
- **1 tablespoon sugar** (optional, adjust to taste)
- **2 green onions**, sliced (for garnish)
- **Shichimi togarashi** (Japanese seven-spice blend) (optional, for added spice)

Instructions:

1. Prepare the Rice:

- **Cook Rice:** Cook the rice according to package instructions. Keep warm.

2. Prepare the Chicken and Sauce:

- **Combine Sauce Ingredients:** In a medium bowl, mix together the dashi stock, soy sauce, mirin, sake (if using), and sugar. Set aside.
- **Cook Chicken and Onions:** In a large skillet or pan, heat a small amount of oil over medium heat. Add the sliced onions and cook until softened, about 3-4 minutes. Add the chicken pieces and cook until they are no longer pink, about 5-7 minutes.
- **Add Sauce:** Pour the sauce mixture over the chicken and onions. Bring to a simmer and cook for another 5 minutes, allowing the flavors to meld and the chicken to cook through.

3. Add Eggs:

- **Beat Eggs:** In a bowl, lightly beat the eggs.
- **Add to Pan:** Gently pour the beaten eggs over the simmering chicken and sauce. Cover the pan with a lid and cook for 2-3 minutes, or until the eggs are just set but still slightly runny. The eggs should be soft and custard-like.

4. Serve:

- **Assemble Bowls:** Spoon a portion of cooked rice into each bowl.
- **Top with Chicken and Egg:** Gently spoon the chicken and egg mixture over the rice.

- **Garnish:** Sprinkle with sliced green onions and a dash of shichimi togarashi if desired.

5. Enjoy:

- **Serve Hot:** Serve the oyakodon hot, straight from the bowl.

Tips:

- **Egg Consistency:** For a creamy texture, make sure not to overcook the eggs. They should remain soft and slightly runny.
- **Rice:** Use short-grain or medium-grain Japanese rice for the best texture, but you can use any type of rice you have on hand.
- **Vegetable Additions:** You can add other vegetables such as mushrooms or bell peppers if desired. Just add them along with the chicken and cook until tender.

Oyakodon is a simple yet flavorful dish that's quick to prepare and perfect for a comforting meal. Its combination of tender chicken, soft eggs, and savory sauce over rice makes it a beloved classic in Japanese cuisine. Enjoy this warm and satisfying meal!

Nikujaga (Japanese Meat and Potato Stew)

Ingredients:

- **1/2 lb (225 g) thinly sliced beef** (such as sirloin or chuck), cut into bite-sized pieces
- **4 medium potatoes**, peeled and cut into bite-sized chunks
- **1 medium onion**, sliced
- **2-3 carrots**, peeled and cut into bite-sized pieces
- **1 cup green beans** (optional), trimmed and cut into 1-inch pieces
- **2 tablespoons vegetable oil**

For the Sauce:

- **1/4 cup soy sauce**
- **1/4 cup mirin**
- **2 tablespoons sugar**
- **1/4 cup sake** (optional)
- **1 cup dashi stock** (or water if dashi is unavailable)

Instructions:

1. Prepare the Ingredients:

- **Cut Vegetables:** Peel and cut the potatoes into chunks. Slice the onion and cut the carrots into bite-sized pieces.
- **Prep Beef:** Cut the beef into bite-sized pieces.

2. Cook the Beef:

- **Heat Oil:** In a large pot or Dutch oven, heat the vegetable oil over medium heat.
- **Brown Beef:** Add the beef and cook until browned on all sides. Remove the beef from the pot and set aside.

3. Cook Vegetables:

- **Sauté Onions:** In the same pot, add the sliced onions and cook until they become translucent, about 3-4 minutes.
- **Add Carrots and Potatoes:** Add the carrots and potatoes to the pot and stir to combine with the onions.

4. Add Sauce Ingredients:

- **Combine Sauce:** In a bowl, mix together the soy sauce, mirin, sugar, sake (if using), and dashi stock.
- **Add to Pot:** Return the browned beef to the pot and pour the sauce mixture over everything. Stir to combine.

5. Simmer the Stew:

- **Bring to Boil:** Bring the mixture to a boil, then reduce the heat to low and cover the pot.
- **Simmer:** Let it simmer gently for about 20-25 minutes, or until the potatoes and carrots are tender and the beef is cooked through. If using green beans, add them in the last 5 minutes of cooking.

6. Serve:

- **Dish Up:** Ladle the Nikujaga into bowls and serve hot.
- **Accompaniment:** Nikujaga is typically served with steamed rice and perhaps a side of pickles.

Tips:

- **Flavor:** The key to Nikujaga's flavor is balancing the sweetness and saltiness of the sauce. Adjust the sugar and soy sauce according to your taste preferences.
- **Vegetables:** Feel free to add other vegetables like mushrooms or bell peppers based on what you have on hand.
- **Texture:** To avoid mushy potatoes, cut them into larger chunks if you prefer them to hold their shape better.

Nikujaga is a comforting and satisfying dish that's easy to make and full of flavor. It's perfect for a family dinner or any time you need a warm, hearty meal. Enjoy this classic Japanese stew!

Zoni (New Year's Mochi Soup)

Ingredients:

- **4 cups dashi stock** (or water if dashi is unavailable)
- **2 tablespoons soy sauce**
- **2 tablespoons mirin**
- **1 tablespoon sake** (optional)
- **1 tablespoon sugar** (optional)
- **1 cup shiitake mushrooms**, sliced
- **1 cup daikon radish**, peeled and sliced into thin rounds
- **1 cup carrot**, peeled and sliced into thin rounds
- **1 cup spinach** or **komatsuna** (Japanese mustard spinach), washed and trimmed
- **1 cup chicken breast** or **thighs**, thinly sliced (or other protein like pork or seafood)
- **4-6 pieces mochi (rice cakes)**, toasted or grilled
- **2 green onions**, sliced (for garnish)
- **Pickled plum** or **kanpyo** (dried gourd strips) (optional, for garnish)
- **Soy sauce** or **salt** to taste

Instructions:

1. Prepare the Broth:

- **Combine Ingredients:** In a large pot, combine the dashi stock, soy sauce, mirin, sake (if using), and sugar (if using). Adjust the seasoning to taste.
- **Heat Broth:** Bring to a gentle simmer over medium heat.

2. Cook the Vegetables and Protein:

- **Add Vegetables:** Add the sliced shiitake mushrooms, daikon radish, and carrot to the pot. Simmer until the vegetables are tender, about 10-15 minutes.
- **Add Protein:** Add the sliced chicken (or other protein) to the pot and cook until the meat is cooked through, about 5-7 minutes.

3. Prepare the Mochi:

- **Toast or Grill Mochi:** Toast or grill the mochi until golden brown and slightly puffed. This can be done under a broiler, on a grill, or in a toaster oven. Alternatively, you can pan-fry them for a crispy texture.

4. Add Greens:

- **Add Spinach:** Stir in the spinach or komatsuna and cook for 1-2 minutes until wilted.

5. Assemble and Serve:

- **Add Mochi:** Divide the toasted mochi into bowls. Ladle the hot soup over the mochi.
- **Garnish:** Garnish with sliced green onions and, if desired, pickled plum or kanpyo.

6. Enjoy:

- **Serve Hot:** Serve the zoni hot and enjoy!

Tips:

- **Flavor:** Adjust the seasoning of the broth to your taste. The sweetness from the mirin and the saltiness from the soy sauce should balance nicely.
- **Mochi:** Ensure the mochi is toasted or grilled well to prevent it from becoming too chewy when added to the soup.
- **Variations:** Ingredients can vary by region. Some versions include other vegetables like taro or different proteins like fish.

Zoni is a warm and hearty soup that embodies the spirit of Japanese New Year's celebrations. It's a dish that brings families together and symbolizes wishes for a prosperous year. Enjoy this traditional and comforting Japanese soup!

Tori Kotsu Ramen (Chicken Bone Ramen)

Ingredients:

For the Broth:

- **4-5 lbs chicken bones** (such as carcasses, wings, or necks)
- **1 onion**, peeled and quartered
- **2-3 garlic cloves**, smashed
- **1-2 inch piece of ginger**, sliced
- **2 green onions**, chopped
- **1-2 carrots**, chopped
- **1 cup white wine** or **sake** (optional, for deglazing)
- **12 cups water** (or enough to cover the bones)
- **Salt**, to taste

For the Ramen:

- **4 servings of fresh or dried ramen noodles**

For Toppings:

- **2 boneless, skinless chicken thighs**, cooked and sliced (or use other meats like chashu)
- **Soft-boiled eggs** (marinated in soy sauce if desired)
- **Bamboo shoots**, sliced
- **Corn kernels** (optional)
- **Bean sprouts** (optional)
- **Nori (seaweed) sheets**
- **Green onions**, sliced
- **Sesame seeds** (optional)
- **Menma (fermented bamboo shoots)** (optional)

Instructions:

1. Prepare the Broth:

- **Blanch the Bones:** In a large pot, cover the chicken bones with cold water. Bring to a boil and then discard the water. This step helps to remove impurities and results in a clearer broth.
- **Simmer the Broth:** Refill the pot with fresh water and add the blanched chicken bones, onion, garlic, ginger, green onions, and carrots. Bring to a boil, then reduce the heat to a simmer.

- **Cook for Richness:** Simmer the broth for 4-6 hours, occasionally skimming off any foam or impurities that rise to the surface. The longer you simmer, the richer and creamier the broth will become.
- **Deglaze (Optional):** If using white wine or sake, add it to the pot during the last 30 minutes of simmering to enhance the flavor.
- **Strain the Broth:** After simmering, strain the broth through a fine-mesh sieve to remove the solids. Season with salt to taste.

2. Prepare the Toppings:

- **Cook Chicken:** Season the chicken thighs with salt and pepper. Pan-fry or grill until cooked through, then slice thinly.
- **Prepare Eggs:** Soft-boil the eggs (cook for 6-7 minutes for a runny yolk). Cool them in ice water, peel, and set aside. For a marinated version, soak them in a mixture of soy sauce and mirin for extra flavor.
- **Prepare Other Toppings:** Prepare and chop any additional toppings such as bamboo shoots, green onions, or nori.

3. Cook the Noodles:

- **Prepare Ramen Noodles:** Cook the ramen noodles according to package instructions. Drain and rinse under cold water to prevent sticking.

4. Assemble the Ramen:

- **Reheat Broth:** Reheat the broth if necessary.
- **Prepare Bowls:** Place cooked noodles into bowls. Ladle hot broth over the noodles.
- **Add Toppings:** Top with sliced chicken, soft-boiled eggs, bamboo shoots, corn, bean sprouts, green onions, and nori. Sprinkle with sesame seeds if desired.

5. Serve:

- **Enjoy:** Serve the ramen hot and enjoy!

Tips:

- **Richness:** For an even richer broth, you can add a small amount of chicken fat (schmaltz) or oil just before serving.
- **Noodles:** Fresh ramen noodles are preferred, but you can use dried noodles if fresh is not available.
- **Broth Storage:** The broth can be made ahead of time and stored in the refrigerator for up to 3 days or frozen for up to 3 months. Skim off any fat that solidifies on top before reheating.

Tori Kotsu Ramen is a delicious and comforting ramen option with a creamy, rich broth that showcases the depth of flavor from chicken bones. It's a great dish to enjoy on a chilly day or whenever you're in the mood for a hearty bowl of ramen.

Karaage (Japanese Fried Chicken)

Ingredients:

- **2 lbs (900 g) boneless, skinless chicken thighs**, cut into bite-sized pieces
- **1/4 cup soy sauce**
- **2 tablespoons sake** (or dry white wine)
- **2 tablespoons mirin** (optional, for a touch of sweetness)
- **1 tablespoon grated ginger**
- **2 garlic cloves**, minced
- **1/4 cup all-purpose flour**
- **1/4 cup cornstarch**
- **1/2 teaspoon baking powder**
- **Salt** and **black pepper**, to taste
- **Vegetable oil** for frying (such as canola or sunflower oil)
- **Lemon wedges** and **shredded cabbage** for serving (optional)

Instructions:

1. Marinate the Chicken:

- **Prepare Marinade:** In a large bowl, mix together the soy sauce, sake, mirin (if using), grated ginger, and minced garlic.
- **Marinate Chicken:** Add the chicken pieces to the marinade, making sure they are well-coated. Cover and refrigerate for at least 30 minutes, or up to 2 hours for deeper flavor.

2. Prepare the Coating:

- **Combine Dry Ingredients:** In a separate bowl, mix together the flour, cornstarch, baking powder, salt, and black pepper.
- **Coat Chicken:** Remove the chicken from the marinade, allowing any excess liquid to drip off. Dredge the chicken pieces in the flour mixture, ensuring they are evenly coated. For extra crispiness, you can double-coat by dipping the chicken back into the marinade and then coating again in the flour mixture.

3. Heat the Oil:

- **Heat Oil:** In a large pot or deep skillet, heat about 2-3 inches of vegetable oil to 350°F (175°C). Use a thermometer to ensure the oil reaches the right temperature for frying.

4. Fry the Chicken:

- **Fry in Batches:** Carefully add the chicken pieces to the hot oil, a few pieces at a time, to avoid overcrowding the pan. Fry for about 4-5 minutes, or until the chicken is golden brown and cooked through.
- **Drain:** Use a slotted spoon to remove the chicken from the oil and transfer it to a paper towel-lined plate to drain excess oil.

5. Serve:

- **Garnish:** Serve the Karaage hot, garnished with lemon wedges and alongside shredded cabbage if desired.

Tips:

- **Marination Time:** For the best flavor, marinate the chicken for at least 30 minutes, but if you have time, marinating overnight is even better.
- **Oil Temperature:** Maintaining the correct oil temperature is crucial for crispy results. If the oil is too hot, the coating may burn before the chicken cooks through. If it's too cool, the chicken may turn out greasy.
- **Coating Variations:** Some recipes use a mix of panko breadcrumbs with the flour for an even crunchier coating.

Karaage is a deliciously crispy and flavorful fried chicken that's perfect for any occasion. Its savory and slightly sweet flavor makes it a standout dish that's sure to please everyone. Enjoy this Japanese favorite!

Tamagoyaki (Japanese Omelette)

Ingredients:

- 4 large eggs
- 2 tablespoons soy sauce
- 2 tablespoons mirin
- 1 tablespoon sugar
- 1 tablespoon vegetable oil (for cooking)

Equipment:

- **Rectangular or square non-stick skillet** (for traditional Tamagoyaki shape)
- **Chopsticks or a spatula**

Instructions:

1. Prepare the Egg Mixture:

- **Beat Eggs:** In a bowl, crack the eggs and beat them lightly with chopsticks or a fork.
- **Add Seasonings:** Add the soy sauce, mirin, and sugar to the eggs. Mix well until the sugar is fully dissolved.

2. Heat the Skillet:

- **Preheat Skillet:** Heat a rectangular or square non-stick skillet over medium-low heat. Brush the skillet with a thin layer of vegetable oil.

3. Cook the Tamagoyaki:

- **First Layer:** Pour a small amount of the egg mixture into the skillet, just enough to cover the bottom of the pan. Tilt the skillet to spread the egg evenly.
- **Cook Until Set:** Let the egg cook until the surface is just set but still slightly wet. Don't let it brown.
- **Roll the Omelette:** Using chopsticks or a spatula, carefully roll the cooked egg layer from one end to the other, forming a log shape. Push the rolled egg to one side of the skillet.
- **Add More Egg Mixture:** Brush the skillet with a little more oil if needed, then pour in another small amount of egg mixture. Lift the rolled egg slightly to let the new layer of egg mixture flow underneath it.
- **Repeat:** Once the new layer is set, roll the omelette again from the end of the previous roll. Continue this process, adding more egg mixture and rolling until all the egg mixture is used.

4. Shape the Tamagoyaki:

- **Final Roll:** When the omelette is fully cooked, let it cook for another minute or two to ensure it's fully set.
- **Transfer and Slice:** Carefully transfer the Tamagoyaki to a cutting board. Let it cool slightly, then slice into pieces. Traditional Tamagoyaki is cut into bite-sized pieces, but you can adjust the size according to your preference.

5. Serve:

- **Presentation:** Serve Tamagoyaki warm or at room temperature. It can be enjoyed on its own, or as part of a sushi roll or bento box.

Tips:

- **Skillet Size:** A rectangular or square skillet is ideal for achieving the traditional shape, but a round skillet will work if that's what you have.
- **Layering:** For a more uniform texture, make sure each layer is thin and well-cooked before adding the next layer.
- **Temperature Control:** Cook the Tamagoyaki over medium-low heat to prevent burning and ensure even cooking.

Tamagoyaki is a versatile and delightful dish that's as pleasing to the eye as it is to the palate. Whether enjoyed as a simple meal or a component of a larger dish, it brings a touch of Japanese elegance to your table.

Miso Katsu (Miso-Glazed Pork Cutlet)

Ingredients:

For the Pork Cutlets:

- **4 pork loin or tenderloin cutlets**, about 1/2 inch thick
- **Salt** and **black pepper**, to taste
- **1/2 cup all-purpose flour**
- **2 large eggs**, beaten
- **1 cup panko breadcrumbs**
- **Vegetable oil**, for frying

For the Miso Sauce:

- **1/4 cup red miso paste**
- **1/4 cup white miso paste**
- **1/4 cup mirin**
- **2 tablespoons soy sauce**
- **2 tablespoons sugar**
- **1 tablespoon sake** (optional)
- **1 tablespoon water** (or as needed to adjust consistency)

Instructions:

1. Prepare the Pork Cutlets:

- **Season Pork:** Season the pork cutlets with salt and black pepper on both sides.
- **Tenderize:** If desired, lightly pound the pork cutlets to even out their thickness and tenderize the meat.

2. Bread the Pork Cutlets:

- **Dredge in Flour:** Coat each cutlet in flour, shaking off excess.
- **Dip in Egg:** Dip the floured cutlet into the beaten eggs, ensuring it is fully coated.
- **Coat with Panko:** Press the cutlet into panko breadcrumbs, covering it evenly. Press gently to help the breadcrumbs adhere.

3. Fry the Pork Cutlets:

- **Heat Oil:** In a large skillet or deep fryer, heat vegetable oil to 350°F (175°C). You need enough oil to submerge the cutlets halfway.
- **Fry Cutlets:** Carefully place the breaded cutlets into the hot oil and fry for 4-5 minutes per side, or until golden brown and cooked through. Adjust the heat as needed to maintain the oil temperature and prevent burning.
- **Drain:** Remove the cutlets from the oil and drain on a paper towel-lined plate.

4. Prepare the Miso Sauce:

- **Combine Ingredients:** In a small saucepan, combine the red miso paste, white miso paste, mirin, soy sauce, sugar, and sake (if using).
- **Cook Sauce:** Cook over medium heat, stirring constantly until the sugar is dissolved and the sauce is smooth. If the sauce is too thick, add water a little at a time to achieve the desired consistency.
- **Simmer:** Simmer the sauce for a few minutes to let the flavors meld together. Remove from heat.

5. Assemble and Serve:

- **Slice Cutlets:** Slice the fried pork cutlets into strips.
- **Glaze with Sauce:** Place the cutlet slices on a serving plate and pour the miso sauce over them. Alternatively, you can serve the sauce on the side for dipping.
- **Garnish:** Garnish with chopped green onions or sesame seeds if desired.

6. Serve:

- **Accompaniment:** Miso Katsu is typically served with steamed rice and shredded cabbage. Pickles or a simple salad can also complement the dish.

Tips:

- **Sauce Consistency:** Adjust the consistency of the miso sauce with water as needed. It should be thick enough to coat the cutlets but not too thick to pour.
- **Frying Temperature:** Maintaining the correct oil temperature is crucial for crispy cutlets. Too hot, and the cutlets might burn; too cool, and they may become greasy.
- **Panko Breadcrumbs:** Use Japanese panko breadcrumbs for the best texture. They create a lighter, crispier coating compared to regular breadcrumbs.

Miso Katsu combines the crispy, savory goodness of traditional Tonkotsu with the rich, umami flavor of miso. It's a comforting and flavorful dish that's sure to be a hit at your table. Enjoy!

Yakiniku (Grilled Meat)

Ingredients:

For the Meat:

- **1 lb (450 g) beef sirloin**, ribeye, or short ribs, thinly sliced
- **1 lb (450 g) pork belly** or **pork shoulder**, thinly sliced
- **1 tablespoon vegetable oil** (for grilling)

For the Marinade:

- **1/4 cup soy sauce**
- **2 tablespoons mirin**
- **2 tablespoons sake** (or dry white wine)
- **2 tablespoons sugar**
- **1 tablespoon grated ginger**
- **1 tablespoon minced garlic**

For Serving:

- **Steamed rice**
- **Shredded cabbage**
- **Grilled vegetables** (e.g., bell peppers, onions, mushrooms)
- **Pickled vegetables** (optional)
- **Yakiniku dipping sauce** (store-bought or homemade)

Instructions:

1. Prepare the Marinade:

- **Mix Marinade Ingredients:** In a bowl, combine the soy sauce, mirin, sake, sugar, grated ginger, and minced garlic. Stir until the sugar is dissolved.

2. Marinate the Meat:

- **Marinate Meat:** Place the thinly sliced meat in a large resealable plastic bag or bowl. Pour the marinade over the meat, ensuring it is well-coated.
- **Refrigerate:** Seal the bag or cover the bowl and refrigerate for at least 30 minutes to 1 hour. For better flavor, marinate overnight.

3. Preheat the Grill:

- **Prepare Grill:** Preheat your charcoal or gas grill to medium-high heat. If using charcoal, let it burn down to a consistent heat.

4. Grill the Meat:

- **Prepare the Grill:** Lightly brush the grill grates with vegetable oil to prevent sticking.
- **Grill Meat:** Remove the meat from the marinade and place it on the grill. Grill the meat for about 1-2 minutes per side, or until it reaches your desired level of doneness. Thin slices cook quickly, so keep an eye on them to avoid overcooking.
- **Grill Vegetables:** If using vegetables, grill them alongside the meat, turning occasionally, until tender and slightly charred.

5. Serve:

- **Arrange the Meal:** Serve the grilled meat and vegetables with steamed rice and shredded cabbage. Provide dipping sauces and pickled vegetables if desired.

6. Dipping Sauce (Optional):

- **Make Yakiniku Sauce:** You can use store-bought yakiniku sauce or make your own by mixing soy sauce, mirin, sake, sugar, and a little sesame oil. Adjust to taste.

Tips:

- **Meat Preparation:** Thinly sliced meat is ideal for yakiniku, allowing for quick grilling and better flavor absorption from the marinade.
- **Grilling Temperature:** Ensure the grill is hot enough to sear the meat and lock in juices. Avoid overcrowding the grill to ensure even cooking.
- **Marinade Variations:** You can add ingredients like sesame seeds, green onions, or chili flakes to the marinade for additional flavors.

Yakiniku is a fun and interactive meal that allows you to customize your grilled meats and vegetables to your taste. It's a great dish for gatherings and can be enjoyed with a variety of side dishes and sauces. Enjoy your delicious Japanese BBQ experience!

Takikomi Gohan (Mixed Rice)

Ingredients:

- **2 cups Japanese short-grain rice** (sushi rice or other short-grain rice)
- **2 1/2 cups dashi stock** (or water with dashi granules)
- **2 tablespoons soy sauce**
- **2 tablespoons mirin**
- **1 tablespoon sake** (optional)
- **1 tablespoon sugar**
- **1/2 cup shiitake mushrooms** (fresh or dried, rehydrated if dried)
- **1/2 cup carrots**, peeled and diced
- **1/2 cup bamboo shoots**, sliced (fresh or canned)
- **1/2 cup chicken thighs** or **pork**, cut into bite-sized pieces (optional)
- **1/2 cup soybeans** or **edamame** (optional)
- **1-2 green onions**, sliced (for garnish)
- **1-2 sheets of nori** (seaweed), shredded (for garnish, optional)

Instructions:

1. Prepare the Ingredients:

- **Rinse Rice:** Rinse the rice under cold water until the water runs clear. This removes excess starch and helps the rice cook evenly.
- **Soak Rice:** Soak the rice in water for about 30 minutes, then drain.

2. Prepare the Vegetables and Meat:

- **Mushrooms:** If using dried shiitake mushrooms, rehydrate them in warm water for 30 minutes. Slice into thin strips.
- **Carrots and Bamboo Shoots:** Peel and dice the carrots into small pieces. Slice bamboo shoots if they're fresh or cut canned bamboo shoots into strips.
- **Meat:** If using meat, cut it into bite-sized pieces and season lightly with salt and pepper.

3. Prepare the Cooking Liquid:

- **Combine Seasonings:** In a bowl, mix the dashi stock, soy sauce, mirin, sake (if using), and sugar.

4. Cook the Takikomi Gohan:

- **Add Ingredients to Rice Cooker or Pot:** Place the soaked and drained rice into the rice cooker or a heavy-bottomed pot. Add the mushrooms, carrots, bamboo shoots, and meat (if using).
- **Pour in Seasoning Liquid:** Pour the seasoning mixture over the ingredients.

- **Cook Rice:** If using a rice cooker, set it to the "Mixed Rice" or "Cook" setting and start. If using a pot, bring the mixture to a boil over medium-high heat, then reduce the heat to low, cover, and simmer for 20-25 minutes, or until the rice is tender and the liquid is absorbed.
- **Rest:** After cooking, let the rice rest with the lid on for 10 minutes to allow the flavors to meld.

5. Serve:

- **Fluff Rice:** Fluff the rice with a fork or rice paddle to mix the ingredients evenly.
- **Garnish:** Garnish with sliced green onions and shredded nori if desired.
- **Enjoy:** Serve hot, either as a main dish or alongside other Japanese dishes.

Tips:

- **Dashi Stock:** If you prefer, you can use store-bought dashi or make it from scratch using kombu (sea kelp) and bonito flakes.
- **Vegetable Variations:** Feel free to customize the vegetables based on what you have on hand or your preferences. Common additions include lotus root, snow peas, or chestnuts.
- **Meat Options:** You can substitute or add other proteins like sliced beef, seafood, or tofu.

Takikomi Gohan is a versatile and flavorful rice dish that's perfect for any meal. The combination of savory ingredients and aromatic seasonings creates a comforting and satisfying dish that highlights the best of Japanese home cooking. Enjoy!

Chashu Pork (Braised Pork Belly)

Ingredients:

- **2 lbs (900 g) pork belly**, skin-on, rolled and tied with kitchen twine
- **1 tablespoon vegetable oil** (for searing)

For the Braising Liquid:

- **1/2 cup soy sauce**
- **1/4 cup sake**
- **1/4 cup mirin**
- **1/4 cup sugar**
- **2 cups water**
- **2 cloves garlic**, smashed
- **1 thumb-sized piece of ginger**, sliced
- **1-2 green onions**, chopped (optional)
- **1 star anise** (optional)

Instructions:

1. Prepare the Pork Belly:

- **Roll and Tie:** If the pork belly isn't already rolled, roll it up tightly and tie it with kitchen twine at regular intervals. This helps it cook evenly and hold its shape.

2. Sear the Pork Belly:

- **Heat Oil:** In a large, heavy-bottomed pot or Dutch oven, heat the vegetable oil over medium-high heat.
- **Sear Pork:** Add the pork belly and sear on all sides until golden brown. This step adds depth of flavor and a nice color to the final dish.

3. Prepare the Braising Liquid:

- **Combine Ingredients:** In a bowl, mix together the soy sauce, sake, mirin, sugar, and water.
- **Add Aromatics:** Add the garlic, ginger, green onions (if using), and star anise (if using) to the mixture.

4. Braise the Pork Belly:

- **Add Liquid:** Pour the braising liquid over the seared pork belly in the pot.
- **Simmer:** Bring the liquid to a boil, then reduce the heat to low. Cover and simmer for 2-3 hours, or until the pork is very tender and easily pulls apart. Turn the pork occasionally to ensure even cooking.

5. Cool and Slice:

- **Cool Pork:** Once the pork is tender, remove it from the braising liquid and let it cool slightly. It's easier to slice when it's a bit cooler.
- **Slice:** Remove the kitchen twine and slice the pork belly into rounds about 1/2 inch thick.

6. Reduce the Sauce (Optional):

- **Thicken Sauce:** If you prefer a thicker sauce, simmer the braising liquid uncovered for an additional 10-15 minutes to reduce and concentrate the flavors. You can brush this sauce over the sliced pork before serving or use it as a dipping sauce.

7. Serve:

- **Use as Topping:** Serve the Chashu Pork as a topping for ramen, rice bowls, or enjoy it on its own with steamed rice or vegetables.

Tips:

- **Marination:** For more intense flavor, you can marinate the pork belly in the braising liquid for a few hours before searing and braising.
- **Flavor Variations:** You can add other spices or ingredients to the braising liquid, such as cinnamon sticks, cloves, or a splash of rice vinegar for added complexity.
- **Storage:** Chashu Pork can be stored in the refrigerator for up to a week or frozen for longer storage. It keeps well and often tastes even better the next day as the flavors continue to develop.

Chashu Pork is a rich, flavorful addition to many dishes, particularly ramen. The slow braising process creates a melt-in-your-mouth texture and deep, savory flavors that are sure to impress. Enjoy your delicious homemade Chashu Pork!

Okonomiyaki (Savory Pancake)

Ingredients:

For the Batter:

- 1 cup all-purpose flour
- 1 cup dashi stock (or water if you don't have dashi)
- 2 large eggs
- 1 cup shredded cabbage
- 1/4 cup thinly sliced green onions
- 1/4 cup grated yam (optional, for extra fluffiness)
- 1/2 cup cooked and chopped bacon (or other preferred protein like pork, shrimp, or squid)

For Toppings and Sauce:

- **Okonomiyaki sauce** (store-bought or homemade, recipe below)
- **Kewpie mayonnaise** (Japanese mayonnaise)
- **Bonito flakes** (katsuobushi)
- **Aonori** (dried seaweed flakes)
- **Pickled ginger** (beni shoga, optional)
- **Thinly sliced green onions** (for garnish)

For Homemade Okonomiyaki Sauce (if not using store-bought):

- 1/4 cup Worcestershire sauce
- 1/4 cup ketchup
- 2 tablespoons soy sauce
- 2 tablespoons mirin
- 1 tablespoon sugar

Instructions:

1. Prepare the Batter:

- **Mix Ingredients:** In a large bowl, whisk together the flour and dashi stock (or water) until smooth.
- **Add Eggs:** Beat in the eggs until fully incorporated.
- **Add Vegetables and Protein:** Fold in the shredded cabbage, green onions, grated yam (if using), and cooked bacon (or other protein). The batter should be thick but pourable.

2. Cook the Okonomiyaki:

- **Preheat the Pan:** Heat a large non-stick skillet or griddle over medium heat. Lightly grease it with vegetable oil or a small amount of melted butter.

- **Pour Batter:** Pour a portion of the batter onto the skillet and spread it into a circle about 1/2 inch thick. You can make one large okonomiyaki or several smaller ones, depending on your preference.
- **Cook:** Cook for about 4-5 minutes until the bottom is golden brown and crispy. Flip carefully and cook the other side for another 4-5 minutes. The pancake should be cooked through and crispy on both sides.

3. Prepare Okonomiyaki Sauce (if making from scratch):

- **Combine Ingredients:** In a small saucepan, combine Worcestershire sauce, ketchup, soy sauce, mirin, and sugar.
- **Simmer:** Cook over medium heat, stirring occasionally, until the sauce is slightly thickened, about 5 minutes. Remove from heat and let cool.

4. Serve:

- **Add Toppings:** Once cooked, transfer the okonomiyaki to a serving plate. Brush with okonomiyaki sauce and drizzle with kewpie mayonnaise.
- **Garnish:** Sprinkle with bonito flakes, aonori, and pickled ginger (if using). Garnish with additional green onions if desired.
- **Slice and Enjoy:** Cut into wedges and serve hot.

Tips:

- **Customizations:** Feel free to add other ingredients like sliced mushrooms, corn, or cheese to the batter. Okonomiyaki is highly customizable, so adjust to your taste.
- **Cooking:** If you're making multiple okonomiyaki, keep them warm in a low oven while you cook the remaining pancakes.
- **Thickness:** For a fluffier okonomiyaki, use a bit of grated yam or a small amount of baking powder in the batter. Adjust the thickness of the pancake based on your preference.

Okonomiyaki is a fun and interactive dish that's perfect for customizing with your favorite ingredients. Whether enjoyed as a main course or as a special treat, it's a delightful representation of Japanese comfort food. Enjoy cooking and eating your homemade okonomiyaki!

Kakuni (Braised Pork Belly)

Ingredients:

- **2 lbs (900 g) pork belly**, cut into 1.5-inch (4 cm) cubes
- **1 tablespoon vegetable oil** (for searing)

For the Braising Liquid:

- **1/4 cup soy sauce**
- **1/4 cup mirin**
- **1/4 cup sake**
- **1/4 cup sugar**
- **1 cup water**
- **2 cloves garlic**, smashed
- **1 thumb-sized piece of ginger**, sliced
- **1-2 green onions**, chopped (optional)
- **1 star anise** (optional)
- **1-2 tablespoons rice vinegar** (optional, for added acidity)

For Garnish (Optional):

- **Thinly sliced green onions**
- **Sesame seeds**

Instructions:

1. Prepare the Pork Belly:

- **Blanch Pork:** In a large pot, cover the pork belly cubes with cold water. Bring to a boil over medium-high heat and cook for about 5 minutes to remove impurities. Drain and rinse the pork belly under cold water.
- **Sear Pork:** Heat the vegetable oil in a large, heavy-bottomed pot or Dutch oven over medium-high heat. Add the pork belly cubes and sear on all sides until browned.

2. Prepare the Braising Liquid:

- **Combine Ingredients:** In a bowl, mix together the soy sauce, mirin, sake, sugar, and water. Stir until the sugar is dissolved.
- **Add Aromatics:** Add the garlic, ginger, green onions (if using), and star anise (if using) to the mixture.

3. Braise the Pork Belly:

- **Add Liquid:** Pour the braising liquid over the seared pork belly in the pot.

- **Simmer:** Bring the liquid to a boil, then reduce the heat to low. Cover and simmer for about 1.5 to 2 hours, or until the pork belly is very tender and can be easily pierced with a fork. Turn the pork occasionally to ensure even cooking.
- **Optional Vinegar:** If desired, add rice vinegar in the last 30 minutes of cooking to balance the flavors and add a slight tang.

4. Reduce the Sauce (Optional):

- **Thicken Sauce:** If you prefer a thicker sauce, remove the pork belly once it's tender and let the braising liquid simmer uncovered for an additional 10-15 minutes until reduced and thickened to your liking. Brush this sauce over the pork before serving or serve it on the side.

5. Serve:

- **Garnish:** Transfer the braised pork belly to a serving plate. Garnish with thinly sliced green onions and sesame seeds if desired.
- **Accompaniment:** Serve with steamed rice, pickled vegetables, or alongside other Japanese dishes.

Tips:

- **Braising Time:** The longer you braise the pork belly, the more tender it will become. Adjust the cooking time based on the size of the pork cubes and your desired tenderness.
- **Flavor Adjustments:** Adjust the sweetness and saltiness of the braising liquid to your taste. You can add more sugar or soy sauce if needed.
- **Storage:** Kakuni can be stored in the refrigerator for up to a week. The flavors often improve after a day or two as it sits in the fridge. It also freezes well for longer storage.

Kakuni is a rich and flavorful dish that highlights the comforting qualities of Japanese braised dishes. The tender, flavorful pork belly combined with a savory-sweet sauce makes for a delightful meal that is sure to impress. Enjoy your homemade Kakuni!

Korokke (Croquettes)

Ingredients:

For the Potato Filling:

- **4 large potatoes**, peeled and cut into chunks
- **1 tablespoon vegetable oil**
- **1/2 onion**, finely chopped
- **1/2 cup cooked ground beef** (or pork, or use mushrooms for a vegetarian option)
- **1/4 cup milk**
- **1/4 cup butter**
- **Salt and pepper**, to taste
- **1/4 teaspoon nutmeg** (optional)
- **1 tablespoon soy sauce** (optional)

For Breading and Frying:

- **1 cup all-purpose flour**
- **2 large eggs**, beaten
- **2 cups panko breadcrumbs**
- **Vegetable oil**, for frying

Instructions:

1. Prepare the Potato Filling:

- **Cook Potatoes:** In a large pot, cover the potato chunks with water and bring to a boil. Cook until tender, about 15-20 minutes. Drain and return to the pot.
- **Mash Potatoes:** Mash the potatoes until smooth. Set aside.
- **Cook Onions and Meat:** In a skillet, heat the vegetable oil over medium heat. Add the chopped onion and cook until translucent. Add the ground meat and cook until browned.
- **Combine Ingredients:** Add the cooked onion and meat mixture to the mashed potatoes. Stir in the milk, butter, salt, pepper, and nutmeg. Mix until well combined and smooth. Adjust seasoning as needed. Allow the mixture to cool.

2. Shape the Korokke:

- **Form Patties:** Once the potato mixture has cooled, shape it into small oval or round patties, about 2-3 inches in diameter and 1/2 inch thick.

3. Bread the Korokke:

- **Prepare Breading Station:** Set up a breading station with three shallow dishes: one with flour, one with beaten eggs, and one with panko breadcrumbs.

- **Bread Patties:** Dredge each patty in flour, coating it evenly. Dip it into the beaten eggs, allowing any excess to drip off. Finally, coat it with panko breadcrumbs, pressing gently to adhere.

4. Fry the Korokke:

- **Heat Oil:** In a large skillet or deep fryer, heat the vegetable oil to 350°F (175°C). Use enough oil to submerge the croquettes.
- **Fry Patties:** Carefully add the breaded patties to the hot oil, a few at a time, without overcrowding the pan. Fry until golden brown and crispy, about 3-4 minutes per side.
- **Drain:** Remove the korokke with a slotted spoon and drain on paper towels.

5. Serve:

- **Enjoy Hot:** Serve the korokke hot, with a side of tonkatsu sauce or your favorite dipping sauce. They're also great with a simple salad or as a part of a larger meal.

Tips:

- **Cooling:** Make sure the potato mixture is completely cool before shaping and breading to prevent it from falling apart during frying.
- **Variation:** You can add vegetables like peas or corn to the filling, or use different meats. For a vegetarian option, use finely chopped mushrooms or a mixture of vegetables.
- **Freezing:** Uncooked korokke can be frozen. Place them on a baking sheet and freeze until solid, then transfer to a freezer bag. Fry from frozen, adding a minute or two to the cooking time.

Korokke are versatile and delicious, perfect as a snack, side dish, or even as a main course. The crispy exterior and flavorful filling make them a favorite in Japanese cuisine. Enjoy making and eating these delightful croquettes!

Katsudon (Pork Cutlet Rice Bowl)

Ingredients:

For the Tonkatsu (Pork Cutlet):

- **4 pork loin chops** or **pork tenderloin**, about 1/2 inch thick
- **Salt and pepper**, to taste
- **1/2 cup all-purpose flour**
- **2 large eggs**, beaten
- **1 cup panko breadcrumbs**
- **Vegetable oil**, for frying

For the Katsudon Sauce:

- **1/2 cup dashi stock** (or water with dashi granules)
- **1/4 cup soy sauce**
- **1/4 cup mirin**
- **2 tablespoons sugar**
- **1 onion**, thinly sliced
- **2 large eggs**

For Serving:

- **4 cups steamed rice**
- **Chopped green onions** (for garnish)
- **Pickled ginger** (optional, for garnish)

Instructions:

1. Prepare the Tonkatsu:

- **Pound Pork:** If the pork chops are thick, pound them gently to an even thickness of about 1/2 inch. This ensures even cooking and helps tenderize the meat.
- **Season Pork:** Season both sides of the pork with salt and pepper.
- **Bread Pork:** Dredge each pork chop in flour, shaking off excess. Dip into the beaten eggs, allowing excess to drip off, then coat thoroughly with panko breadcrumbs.
- **Fry Pork:** Heat about 1/2 inch of vegetable oil in a large skillet over medium-high heat. Fry the pork cutlets for 3-4 minutes per side, or until golden brown and cooked through. Remove and drain on paper towels. Slice each cutlet into strips.

2. Prepare the Katsudon Sauce:

- **Combine Sauce Ingredients:** In a medium bowl, mix the dashi stock, soy sauce, mirin, and sugar. Stir until the sugar is dissolved.

- **Cook Onions:** In a skillet or shallow pan, heat a small amount of oil over medium heat. Add the sliced onions and cook until softened and slightly caramelized, about 5 minutes.
- **Add Sauce:** Pour the sauce mixture over the onions and bring to a simmer.
- **Add Eggs:** Gently place the sliced pork cutlets into the simmering sauce, arranging them in a single layer. Pour the beaten eggs over the pork and cover. Cook for about 2-3 minutes, or until the eggs are just set. The eggs should be soft and slightly runny.

3. Assemble the Katsudon:

- **Prepare Rice:** Divide the steamed rice among four bowls.
- **Top with Tonkatsu:** Spoon the pork cutlet and sauce mixture over the rice in each bowl.
- **Garnish:** Garnish with chopped green onions and pickled ginger if desired.

4. Serve:

- **Enjoy Hot:** Serve the Katsudon hot. It's best enjoyed immediately while the rice is warm and the cutlet is still crispy.

Tips:

- **Dashi Stock:** Using dashi stock adds a rich umami flavor to the sauce, but you can substitute with water if you don't have dashi granules or stock.
- **Eggs:** For a more traditional Katsudon, cook the eggs just until they are set but still a bit runny. This adds a creamy texture to the dish.
- **Tonkatsu Variations:** You can also use chicken or other proteins instead of pork for variations of this dish.

Katsudon is a beloved Japanese comfort food, offering a perfect blend of savory pork, sweet and salty sauce, and tender rice. It's a satisfying and flavorful dish that's sure to please any palate. Enjoy your homemade Katsudon!

Goya Champuru (Bitter Melon Stir-Fry)

Ingredients:

- **1 large bitter melon (goya)**
- **1 block (14 oz) firm tofu**, drained and cubed
- **1/2 lb (225 g) pork belly** or pork loin, thinly sliced (you can substitute with chicken or leave it out for a vegetarian option)
- **2 tablespoons vegetable oil**
- **2-3 cloves garlic**, minced
- **1 small onion**, thinly sliced
- **2 tablespoons soy sauce**
- **1 tablespoon mirin** (optional, for a touch of sweetness)
- **1 tablespoon sake** (optional, for added flavor)
- **Salt and pepper**, to taste
- **Red pepper flakes** or **shichimi togarashi** (optional, for added spice)
- **Chopped green onions** (for garnish)
- **Sesame seeds** (for garnish)

Instructions:

1. Prepare the Bitter Melon:

- **Slice Melon:** Cut the bitter melon in half lengthwise and scoop out the seeds with a spoon. Slice the melon into thin half-moon shapes.
- **Salt Melon:** Sprinkle the sliced bitter melon with salt and let it sit for about 10 minutes. This helps reduce the bitterness. Rinse thoroughly and pat dry with paper towels.

2. Prepare the Tofu:

- **Press Tofu:** Place the tofu between paper towels and press gently to remove excess moisture.
- **Cube Tofu:** Cut the tofu into bite-sized cubes.

3. Cook the Pork:

- **Heat Oil:** In a large skillet or wok, heat the vegetable oil over medium heat.
- **Cook Pork:** Add the sliced pork and cook until browned and cooked through, about 5 minutes. Remove the pork from the skillet and set aside.

4. Cook the Tofu:

- **Fry Tofu:** In the same skillet, add a bit more oil if needed. Add the tofu cubes and cook until golden brown on all sides, about 5-7 minutes. Remove and set aside with the cooked pork.

5. Stir-Fry Vegetables:

- **Cook Aromatics:** In the same skillet, add the minced garlic and sliced onion. Cook until the onion is translucent and fragrant, about 2 minutes.
- **Add Bitter Melon:** Add the sliced bitter melon to the skillet. Stir-fry for about 5-7 minutes until the melon is tender but still slightly crisp.

6. Combine Ingredients:

- **Return Pork and Tofu:** Add the cooked pork and tofu back into the skillet with the bitter melon.
- **Season:** Add the soy sauce, mirin (if using), and sake (if using). Stir well to combine and heat through. Season with salt, pepper, and red pepper flakes or shichimi togarashi if desired.

7. Serve:

- **Garnish:** Transfer the Goya Champuru to a serving plate or bowl. Garnish with chopped green onions and sesame seeds.
- **Enjoy:** Serve hot with steamed rice or as part of a larger meal.

Tips:

- **Reduce Bitterness:** If you find the bitter melon too bitter even after salting, you can blanch it briefly in boiling water before using it in the stir-fry.
- **Tofu Texture:** For a firmer texture, use extra-firm tofu. You can also press the tofu for longer to remove more moisture.
- **Vegetarian Option:** For a vegetarian version, you can omit the pork and use mushrooms or other vegetables as a substitute.

Goya Champuru is a flavorful and nutritious dish that highlights the unique taste of bitter melon. Its combination of textures and flavors makes it a standout recipe in Okinawan cuisine. Enjoy preparing and eating this distinctive and delicious stir-fry!

Soba Noodle Soup

Ingredients:

For the Broth:

- **4 cups dashi stock** (or substitute with chicken or vegetable broth)
- **1/4 cup soy sauce**
- **2 tablespoons mirin**
- **1 tablespoon sake** (optional)
- **1 tablespoon sugar** (optional, for a touch of sweetness)
- **1-2 tablespoons miso** (optional, for additional depth of flavor)

For the Soup:

- **8 oz (225 g) soba noodles**
- **1 cup sliced mushrooms** (shiitake, cremini, or any kind you prefer)
- **1 cup sliced green onions**
- **1 cup baby spinach** or other greens (like bok choy or kale)
- **1 medium carrot**, julienned
- **1/2 cup sliced daikon radish** (optional)
- **1/2 cup tofu**, cubed (optional)
- **1/2 cup cooked chicken** or other protein (optional)

Garnishes (Optional):

- **Nori seaweed**, cut into strips
- **Sesame seeds**
- **Pickled ginger**
- **Chili flakes** or **shichimi togarashi** (for heat)

Instructions:

1. Prepare the Broth:

- **Combine Ingredients:** In a large pot, combine the dashi stock, soy sauce, mirin, and sake (if using). Stir well.
- **Simmer:** Bring the mixture to a simmer over medium heat. If using miso, dissolve it in a small amount of warm broth and then stir it back into the pot. Simmer for 5-10 minutes, adjusting seasoning to taste.

2. Cook the Soba Noodles:

- **Boil Noodles:** In a separate pot, bring water to a boil and cook the soba noodles according to the package instructions, usually 4-5 minutes. Drain and rinse under cold water to remove excess starch.

3. Prepare the Vegetables and Tofu:

- **Cook Vegetables:** In a skillet or wok, heat a small amount of oil over medium heat. Add the mushrooms, carrot, and daikon radish (if using). Stir-fry until tender, about 5 minutes.
- **Add Tofu:** If using tofu, add it to the skillet and cook for an additional 2-3 minutes until warmed through.

4. Combine and Serve:

- **Add Vegetables to Broth:** Add the stir-fried vegetables and tofu to the simmering broth. If using cooked chicken, add it now as well. Simmer for an additional 5 minutes.
- **Add Greens:** Stir in the greens and cook for another 1-2 minutes until wilted.

5. Assemble the Soup:

- **Prepare Bowls:** Divide the cooked soba noodles among serving bowls.
- **Add Broth and Toppings:** Ladle the hot broth, vegetables, and tofu over the noodles in each bowl.

6. Garnish and Serve:

- **Add Garnishes:** Top with nori strips, sesame seeds, pickled ginger, or chili flakes if desired.
- **Enjoy:** Serve the Soba Noodle Soup hot, and enjoy!

Tips:

- **Adjusting Broth:** You can adjust the saltiness of the broth by adding more or less soy sauce. If the broth is too salty, you can dilute it with a bit of water or more dashi.
- **Protein Options:** Besides tofu and chicken, you can also use other proteins like shrimp or pork if preferred.
- **Vegetable Variations:** Feel free to customize the vegetables based on what you have on hand or your personal preferences.

Soba Noodle Soup is versatile and can be adapted to different tastes and ingredients, making it a great option for a warm and nourishing meal. Enjoy making and savoring this delicious Japanese soup!

Butajiru (Pork and Vegetable Miso Soup)

Ingredients:

- **200 g (7 oz) pork belly** or **pork shoulder**, thinly sliced
- **1 tablespoon vegetable oil**
- **1 medium onion**, sliced
- **2 carrots**, peeled and sliced into half-moons
- **1 medium daikon radish**, peeled and sliced
- **1 cup potatoes**, peeled and diced
- **2-3 green onions**, chopped
- **1 block (14 oz) firm tofu**, cubed
- **4 cups dashi stock** (or substitute with chicken or vegetable broth)
- **3-4 tablespoons miso paste** (white or red miso)
- **1 tablespoon soy sauce** (optional, for extra seasoning)
- **Salt and pepper**, to taste

Instructions:

1. Prepare the Ingredients:

- **Slice Pork:** Thinly slice the pork belly or pork shoulder into bite-sized pieces.
- **Prepare Vegetables:** Slice the onion, carrots, daikon radish, and dice the potatoes. Cube the tofu.

2. Cook the Pork:

- **Heat Oil:** In a large pot, heat the vegetable oil over medium heat.
- **Brown Pork:** Add the sliced pork and cook until it starts to brown and is no longer pink. Remove the pork from the pot and set aside.

3. Cook the Vegetables:

- **Sauté Onions:** In the same pot, add the sliced onion and cook until softened and translucent.
- **Add Vegetables:** Add the carrots, daikon radish, and potatoes. Cook for a few minutes, stirring occasionally.

4. Add Broth and Simmer:

- **Add Dashi Stock:** Pour in the dashi stock (or substitute broth) and bring to a boil.
- **Simmer:** Reduce heat and let it simmer for about 10-15 minutes, or until the vegetables are tender.

5. Add Pork and Tofu:

- **Return Pork:** Add the browned pork back into the pot.
- **Add Tofu:** Gently stir in the cubed tofu.

6. Season the Soup:

- **Dissolve Miso:** In a small bowl, ladle some hot broth from the pot and dissolve the miso paste in it. Stir until smooth. Then return the miso mixture to the pot.
- **Season:** Taste and adjust seasoning with soy sauce (if using), salt, and pepper.

7. Finish and Serve:

- **Add Green Onions:** Stir in the chopped green onions.
- **Serve Hot:** Ladle the soup into bowls and serve hot.

Tips:

- **Adjusting Miso:** Depending on the type of miso and your taste preference, you can adjust the amount of miso paste. Start with less and add more to taste.
- **Vegetable Variations:** You can use other vegetables like mushrooms, bell peppers, or cabbage according to your preference or seasonal availability.
- **Protein Options:** If you prefer a lighter version, you can use chicken or omit the meat entirely for a vegetarian option.

Butajiru is a flavorful and filling soup that's perfect for a cozy meal. Its combination of pork, vegetables, and miso makes it a hearty and nutritious dish that's loved across Japan. Enjoy making and savoring this delicious soup!

Kuri Gohan (Chestnut Rice)

Ingredients:

- **1 cup short-grain Japanese rice** (such as sushi rice or koshihikari)
- **1 cup chestnuts**, peeled and cooked (see note for how to prepare)
- **1 1/2 cups dashi stock** (or water if you prefer)
- **1 tablespoon soy sauce**
- **1 tablespoon mirin**
- **1/2 teaspoon salt**
- **1-2 tablespoons sake** (optional)
- **Chopped green onions** (for garnish, optional)

Instructions:

1. Prepare the Chestnuts:

- **Peel Chestnuts:** If using fresh chestnuts, score the shell with a knife and boil or roast them to make peeling easier. Once peeled, the chestnuts should be soft and slightly sweet. If using canned or pre-cooked chestnuts, drain and chop them into pieces.
- **Cut Chestnuts:** For uniform cooking, cut the chestnuts into halves or quarters.

2. Prepare the Rice:

- **Rinse Rice:** Place the rice in a sieve or bowl and rinse under cold water until the water runs clear. This removes excess starch and helps achieve a fluffy texture.
- **Soak Rice:** Soak the rinsed rice in water for about 30 minutes to 1 hour. Drain well before cooking.

3. Cook the Rice:

- **Combine Ingredients:** In a rice cooker or a heavy-bottomed pot, combine the soaked rice, dashi stock (or water), soy sauce, mirin, and salt. Add the sake if using.
- **Add Chestnuts:** Gently stir in the chopped chestnuts.

4. Cook the Rice:

- **Rice Cooker:** If using a rice cooker, set it to the "Cook" function and let it do its job. The rice cooker will automatically switch to "Keep Warm" once the rice is done.
- **Pot Method:** If cooking on the stovetop, bring the mixture to a boil over medium-high heat. Once it starts boiling, reduce the heat to low, cover with a lid, and let it simmer for about 15-20 minutes. Turn off the heat and let it sit, covered, for an additional 10 minutes to allow the rice to finish steaming.

5. Fluff and Serve:

- **Fluff Rice:** After the rice is done cooking, gently fluff it with a rice paddle or fork to separate the grains and distribute the chestnuts evenly.
- **Garnish:** Garnish with chopped green onions if desired.

6. Serve:

- **Enjoy:** Serve the Kuri Gohan warm as a main or side dish.

Tips:

- **Chestnut Preparation:** If using fresh chestnuts, make sure to peel them thoroughly. You can use pre-cooked chestnuts to save time.
- **Rice Texture:** For best results, use short-grain Japanese rice, which has a stickier texture that complements the chestnuts.
- **Flavor Adjustments:** Adjust the amount of soy sauce and mirin according to your taste preference. If you like a slightly sweeter rice, you can add a bit more mirin.

Kuri Gohan is a delicious and seasonal dish that highlights the unique flavor of chestnuts. Its nutty and slightly sweet taste makes it a comforting choice for autumn and winter meals. Enjoy preparing and savoring this traditional Japanese recipe!

Kiritanpo Nabe (Rice Stick Hot Pot)

Ingredients:

For the Broth:

- **4 cups dashi stock** (or substitute with chicken or vegetable broth)
- **1/4 cup soy sauce**
- **1/4 cup mirin**
- **2 tablespoons sake**
- **1-2 tablespoons miso** (optional, for additional flavor)

For the Hot Pot:

- **8-10 kiritanpo rice sticks** (you can use store-bought kiritanpo or make your own; see note below)
- **1/2 lb (225 g) chicken thighs**, cut into bite-sized pieces
- **1 cup mushrooms** (shiitake, enoki, or any variety you prefer)
- **1 cup Chinese cabbage** or napa cabbage, chopped
- **1 cup sliced carrots**
- **1 cup daikon radish**, sliced
- **1 cup tofu**, cubed (optional)
- **1-2 green onions**, sliced
- **1-2 tablespoons vegetable oil** (for cooking)

Garnishes (Optional):

- **Chopped green onions**
- **Sesame seeds**
- **Shichimi togarashi** (for added spice)

Instructions:

1. Prepare the Kiritanpo:

- **Make Rice Sticks:** If you're making your own kiritanpo, cook short-grain rice as you normally would, then form it into cylindrical sticks while the rice is still warm. Grill or toast them until slightly crispy on the outside. If using store-bought kiritanpo, just cut them to the desired size.

2. Prepare the Broth:

- **Combine Ingredients:** In a large pot, combine the dashi stock, soy sauce, mirin, and sake. If using miso, dissolve it in a small amount of warm broth and stir it into the pot.
- **Simmer:** Bring the broth to a simmer over medium heat and let it cook for about 10 minutes to meld the flavors.

3. Prepare the Hot Pot Ingredients:

- **Cook Chicken:** In a separate skillet or the same pot, heat a small amount of vegetable oil over medium heat. Add the chicken pieces and cook until browned and cooked through. Remove and set aside.
- **Sauté Vegetables:** In the same pot, sauté the mushrooms, carrots, daikon radish, and any other vegetables you're using until slightly tender.

4. Assemble the Hot Pot:

- **Combine Ingredients:** Add the sautéed vegetables, cooked chicken, and kiritanpo rice sticks to the simmering broth. Add the tofu if using.
- **Simmer:** Continue to simmer the hot pot for about 10-15 minutes, or until the vegetables are tender and the kiritanpo is heated through.

5. Serve:

- **Garnish:** Ladle the hot pot into bowls and garnish with sliced green onions, sesame seeds, and shichimi togarashi if desired.
- **Enjoy:** Serve hot and enjoy the comforting flavors of this Japanese nabe dish.

Tips:

- **Kiritanpo:** If you cannot find kiritanpo, you can use cooked rice cakes (such as those used in other Japanese dishes) or even plain steamed rice formed into sticks.
- **Broth Adjustments:** Adjust the amount of soy sauce and mirin based on your taste preference. For a richer flavor, you can add more soy sauce or miso.
- **Vegetable Variations:** Feel free to customize the vegetables according to what you have on hand or what you enjoy.

Kiritanpo Nabe is a heartwarming and delicious hot pot dish that brings together the flavors of grilled rice sticks, tender chicken, and a savory broth. It's perfect for sharing with family or friends on a cold day. Enjoy making and eating this traditional Japanese comfort food!

Satsuma Age (Deep-Fried Fish Cake)

Ingredients:

- **300 g (10 oz) white fish fillets** (such as cod, haddock, or tilapia)
- **1/2 cup (60 g) finely chopped onions**
- **1/2 cup (60 g) finely chopped carrots**
- **1/4 cup (30 g) finely chopped green onions**
- **2 tablespoons soy sauce**
- **1 tablespoon mirin**
- **1 tablespoon sake**
- **1 teaspoon sugar**
- **1 egg white**
- **2 tablespoons potato starch** or cornstarch
- **Salt and pepper**, to taste
- **Vegetable oil** (for frying)

Instructions:

1. Prepare the Fish:

- **Process Fish:** Place the fish fillets in a food processor and pulse until finely ground. You can also chop the fish finely by hand if you don't have a food processor.

2. Mix Ingredients:

- **Combine Ingredients:** In a large bowl, combine the ground fish, chopped onions, carrots, and green onions.
- **Season:** Add the soy sauce, mirin, sake, sugar, salt, and pepper. Mix well.
- **Bind Mixture:** Add the egg white and potato starch (or cornstarch) to the mixture. Stir until the mixture is well combined and slightly sticky.

3. Form the Fish Cakes:

- **Shape Mixture:** Wet your hands slightly to prevent sticking. Shape the fish mixture into small patties or oval shapes, about 1/2-inch thick.

4. Fry the Fish Cakes:

- **Heat Oil:** In a deep skillet or frying pan, heat vegetable oil over medium heat to about 350°F (180°C). You need enough oil to cover the fish cakes halfway.
- **Fry Cakes:** Fry the fish cakes in batches, being careful not to overcrowd the pan. Cook for 3-4 minutes on each side, or until golden brown and crispy.
- **Drain:** Remove the fish cakes from the oil and drain on paper towels.

5. Serve:

- **Enjoy:** Serve hot or at room temperature. Satsuma Age can be enjoyed on its own, with a dipping sauce, or as part of a larger meal.

Tips:

- **Fish Variety:** Use firm white fish for best results. Fresh fish will yield the best texture, but frozen fish can also be used if thawed properly.
- **Vegetables:** You can add other finely chopped vegetables like bell peppers or mushrooms according to your preference.
- **Texture:** The addition of potato starch or cornstarch helps in achieving a lighter and fluffier texture for the fish cakes.

Satsuma Age is a delightful treat that's crispy on the outside and tender on the inside. It's perfect for serving as a snack, appetizer, or a side dish. Enjoy making and savoring this tasty Japanese delicacy!

Yudofu (Tofu Hot Pot)

Ingredients

- **Silken or soft tofu**: Cut into large cubes
- **Dashi**: A Japanese soup stock, often made from kombu (kelp) and bonito flakes. You can buy it pre-made or make your own.
- **Shiitake mushrooms**: Sliced
- **Leafy greens**: Like spinach or bok choy
- **Green onions**: Chopped
- **Soy sauce**: For seasoning
- **Mirin**: A sweet rice wine
- **Optional**: Carrots, enoki mushrooms, or other vegetables
- **Optional condiments**: Soy sauce, ponzu sauce, or sesame sauce for dipping

Instructions

1. **Prepare the Dashi**: If you're using instant dashi, dissolve it in hot water according to the package instructions. If you're making it from scratch, simmer kombu and bonito flakes in water, then strain out the solids.
2. **Prepare the Tofu and Vegetables**: Cut the tofu into large cubes. Clean and slice your vegetables.
3. **Heat the Broth**: In a pot, bring the dashi to a simmer.
4. **Add Vegetables**: Start with harder vegetables like carrots and mushrooms. Let them cook until they're just tender.
5. **Add Tofu**: Gently add the tofu cubes and let them heat through. Be careful not to stir too vigorously, as tofu can break apart easily.
6. **Season**: Add a splash of soy sauce and a bit of mirin to taste.
7. **Serve**: Transfer everything to a serving bowl or pot at the table. Serve with additional dipping sauces if desired.

Tips

- **Freshness**: Using high-quality tofu and fresh dashi makes a big difference.
- **Garnishes**: Freshly chopped green onions or a sprinkle of sesame seeds can add a nice touch.

Yudofu is great on a chilly day or as a light, warming meal. Enjoy your cozy hot pot!

Buta Kakuni (Braised Pork Belly)

Ingredients

- **Pork belly**: 500-700 grams (about 1 pound), cut into 1.5-inch cubes
- **Ginger**: 1-inch piece, sliced
- **Garlic**: 2-3 cloves, smashed
- **Green onions**: 2-3, cut into large pieces
- **Soy sauce**: 1/4 cup
- **Mirin**: 1/4 cup
- **Sake**: 1/4 cup
- **Sugar**: 2 tablespoons (white or brown sugar works)
- **Water**: Enough to cover the pork
- **Optional**: Star anise or a cinnamon stick for additional flavor

Instructions

1. **Blanch the Pork Belly**: Place the pork belly cubes in a pot of cold water. Bring to a boil over high heat and cook for 2-3 minutes. This step helps remove impurities and excess fat. Drain and rinse the pork belly under cold water.
2. **Prepare the Braising Liquid**: In a separate pot, combine soy sauce, mirin, sake, and sugar. Stir until the sugar is dissolved.
3. **Sear the Pork Belly**: Heat a little oil in a heavy-bottomed pot or Dutch oven over medium-high heat. Add the blanched pork belly cubes and sear them until browned on all sides. This step adds depth of flavor to the dish.
4. **Add Aromatics**: Once the pork belly is browned, add the sliced ginger, smashed garlic, and green onions. Stir briefly to combine.
5. **Add Braising Liquid**: Pour the prepared braising liquid over the pork belly. Add enough water to just cover the pork. If using, add star anise or a cinnamon stick at this point.
6. **Simmer**: Bring the liquid to a boil, then reduce the heat to low. Cover the pot and let it simmer gently for 1.5 to 2 hours, or until the pork is tender and the flavors have melded together. Occasionally check and skim off any excess fat that rises to the surface.
7. **Reduce the Sauce (Optional)**: If you prefer a thicker sauce, remove the pork belly once it's tender and continue to simmer the sauce until it reduces to your desired consistency. Then return the pork to the pot.
8. **Serve**: Serve the Buta Kakuni hot, with steamed rice or as part of a larger meal. It pairs wonderfully with vegetables like bok choy or pickled ginger.

Tips

- **Marination**: For even more flavor, you can marinate the pork belly in the soy sauce, mirin, and sake mixture for a few hours before braising.
- **Skimming Fat**: During simmering, regularly skim off any excess fat to keep the dish from being too greasy.

- **Refrigeration**: Buta Kakuni often tastes even better the next day after the flavors have had more time to meld.

Enjoy making and savoring this rich and savory dish!

Niku Miso (Meat Miso)

Ingredients

- **Ground meat**: 250 grams (about 1/2 pound) of pork, beef, or a mix
- **Miso paste**: 3-4 tablespoons (red or white miso)
- **Garlic**: 2-3 cloves, minced
- **Ginger**: 1-inch piece, minced
- **Onion**: 1 medium, finely chopped
- **Carrot**: 1 small, finely diced (optional)
- **Soy sauce**: 1-2 tablespoons
- **Sake**: 1 tablespoon (optional)
- **Mirin**: 1 tablespoon (optional)
- **Vegetable oil**: 1-2 tablespoons for cooking
- **Green onions**: Chopped, for garnish (optional)
- **Sesame seeds**: For garnish (optional)

Instructions

1. **Heat the Oil**: In a large skillet or pan, heat the vegetable oil over medium heat.
2. **Cook the Aromatics**: Add the minced garlic and ginger to the pan. Sauté for about 1 minute until fragrant.
3. **Add the Onions and Carrots**: Add the finely chopped onion (and carrot, if using) to the pan. Cook until the onions are translucent and the carrots are tender, about 5-7 minutes.
4. **Brown the Meat**: Add the ground meat to the pan. Cook until it's browned and fully cooked, breaking it up into small pieces with a spatula.
5. **Incorporate the Miso Paste**: Stir in the miso paste, making sure it's well mixed with the meat and vegetables.
6. **Add Seasonings**: Add the soy sauce, sake, and mirin if using. Stir to combine and let the mixture simmer for another 5 minutes to allow the flavors to meld. Taste and adjust seasoning if necessary.
7. **Finish and Serve**: Garnish with chopped green onions and sesame seeds if desired.

Serving Suggestions

- **Rice**: Spoon the Niku Miso over steamed white rice or brown rice.
- **Noodles**: Use it as a topping for soba, udon, or ramen noodles.
- **Vegetables**: Serve with steamed or sautéed vegetables.
- **Dumplings**: Use as a filling for gyoza or other dumplings.

Tips

- **Miso Variety**: Red miso will give a richer, stronger flavor, while white miso is milder and sweeter. You can adjust based on your taste preference.

- **Texture**: For a smoother texture, you can finely chop or process the vegetables.
- **Storage**: Niku Miso can be stored in the refrigerator for up to a week or frozen for longer storage.

Enjoy your savory, umami-packed Niku Miso!

Shoyu Ramen (Soy Sauce Ramen)

Ingredients

For the Broth:

- **Chicken or pork bones**: 500 grams (about 1 pound), preferably with some meat on them
- **Water**: Enough to cover the bones
- **Ginger**: 1-inch piece, sliced
- **Garlic**: 2-3 cloves, smashed
- **Green onions**: 2-3, cut into large pieces
- **Shiitake mushrooms**: 3-4, dried or fresh
- **Soy sauce**: 1/4 cup
- **Mirin**: 2 tablespoons
- **Sake**: 2 tablespoons (optional)
- **Salt**: To taste

For the Toppings:

- **Ramen noodles**: 4 servings, cooked according to package instructions
- **Chashu pork**: Slices (recipe below) or store-bought
- **Soft-boiled eggs**: 4, marinated (recipe below)
- **Nori (seaweed)**: Sheets, cut into strips
- **Green onions**: Chopped
- **Bamboo shoots**: Sliced, pickled (optional)
- **Bean sprouts**: Lightly blanched (optional)
- **Corn**: Fresh or frozen (optional)

Instructions

Broth Preparation:

1. **Prepare the Bones**: Rinse the chicken or pork bones under cold water. Place them in a large pot and cover with cold water. Bring to a boil over high heat. Once boiling, discard the water and rinse the bones. This step helps remove impurities and results in a clearer broth.
2. **Simmer the Broth**: Return the bones to the pot and add fresh water to cover. Add ginger, garlic, green onions, and shiitake mushrooms. Bring to a boil, then reduce the heat to low. Simmer for 2-3 hours, skimming off any foam or fat that rises to the surface.
3. **Season the Broth**: After simmering, strain the broth through a fine-mesh sieve into another pot. Discard the solids. Stir in soy sauce, mirin, and sake if using. Taste and adjust salt as needed.

Chashu Pork (Optional):

1. **Ingredients**: 500 grams (about 1 pound) pork belly, soy sauce, mirin, sake, sugar, and water.
2. **Prepare**: Roll the pork belly into a log and tie with kitchen twine.
3. **Cook**: Sear the pork in a hot pan until browned on all sides. Add soy sauce, mirin, sake, sugar, and enough water to cover the pork. Simmer for 2-3 hours or until tender. Slice thinly once cooled.

Soft-Boiled Eggs (Marinated):

1. **Ingredients**: 4 large eggs, soy sauce, mirin, and a little sugar.
2. **Cook**: Boil the eggs for 7 minutes for a slightly runny yolk or 8 minutes for a firmer yolk. Cool in ice water.
3. **Marinate**: Peel the eggs and marinate in a mixture of soy sauce, mirin, and a little sugar for at least 1 hour or overnight in the refrigerator.

Assembly:

1. **Prepare Noodles**: Cook the ramen noodles according to package instructions. Drain and divide among bowls.
2. **Add Broth**: Pour the hot broth over the noodles in each bowl.
3. **Top**: Add slices of chashu pork, halved marinated eggs, nori strips, green onions, and any additional toppings you like such as bamboo shoots, bean sprouts, or corn.
4. **Serve**: Enjoy your homemade Shoyu Ramen while hot!

Tips

- **Broth Clarity**: Blanching the bones before simmering helps keep the broth clear.
- **Toppings**: Customize the toppings based on your preference or what you have on hand.
- **Noodles**: Fresh ramen noodles are ideal, but you can use dried noodles if that's what you have.

Enjoy your delicious bowl of Shoyu Ramen!

Oden (Winter Stew)

Ingredients

For the Broth:

- **Dashi**: 4 cups (you can use instant dashi or make your own with kombu and bonito flakes)
- **Soy sauce**: 1/4 cup
- **Mirin**: 2 tablespoons
- **Sugar**: 1-2 tablespoons (adjust to taste)
- **Sake**: 2 tablespoons (optional)

For the Stew:

- **Daikon radish**: 1, peeled and cut into thick slices
- **Carrots**: 1-2, peeled and cut into chunks
- **Konnyaku**: 1 package, sliced into triangles or strips
- **Tofu**: 1 block, cut into cubes (fried tofu or regular tofu)
- **Boiled eggs**: 4-6, peeled
- **Fish cakes**: Various types (like chikuwa, satsuma-age, or kamaboko)
- **Other additions**: Optional items like meatballs, chicken wings, or mushrooms

Instructions

1. **Prepare the Dashi**:
    - **Instant Dashi**: Dissolve according to package instructions.
    - **Homemade Dashi**: Simmer kombu (dried kelp) in water, then add bonito flakes and strain.
2. **Prepare the Ingredients**:
    - **Daikon Radish**: Simmer in water until tender. This usually takes about 15-20 minutes.
    - **Carrots**: Cook until tender, about 10-15 minutes.
    - **Konnyaku**: Boil for a few minutes to remove any odor. Slice into triangles or strips.
    - **Tofu**: If using regular tofu, lightly pan-fry or grill to give it some texture.
    - **Boiled Eggs**: Boil eggs for 7-8 minutes, then peel.
3. **Make the Broth**:
    - In a large pot, combine the dashi, soy sauce, mirin, sugar, and sake (if using). Bring to a gentle simmer.
4. **Cook the Ingredients**:
    - Add the daikon, carrots, and konnyaku to the pot. Simmer for about 10 minutes.
    - Add the tofu, fish cakes, and boiled eggs. Continue to simmer for an additional 10-15 minutes, allowing all the ingredients to absorb the flavors of the broth.
5. **Serve**:

- Ladle the oden into bowls, making sure each serving gets a variety of ingredients.
- Serve hot, often with a side of mustard for dipping, if desired.

Tips

- **Flavor Development**: Oden often tastes even better the next day after the flavors have had more time to meld together.
- **Variations**: You can customize your oden with other ingredients like mushrooms, meatballs, or additional fish cakes based on your preferences.
- **Storage**: Store leftovers in the refrigerator for up to a week, and it can be reheated on the stove.

Enjoy making and savoring your warm, comforting bowl of Oden!

Miso Ramen

Ingredients

For the Broth:

- **Chicken or pork bones**: 500 grams (about 1 pound), preferably with some meat on them
- **Water**: Enough to cover the bones
- **Dashi**: 4 cups (optional, for extra depth of flavor; can use instant dashi or homemade)
- **Miso paste**: 1/4 cup (white or red miso, or a mix)
- **Soy sauce**: 2 tablespoons
- **Mirin**: 2 tablespoons
- **Sake**: 2 tablespoons (optional)
- **Garlic**: 2-3 cloves, minced
- **Ginger**: 1-inch piece, minced
- **Green onions**: 2-3, chopped

For the Toppings:

- **Ramen noodles**: 4 servings, cooked according to package instructions
- **Chashu pork**: Slices (recipe below) or store-bought
- **Soft-boiled eggs**: 4, marinated (recipe below)
- **Corn**: Fresh or frozen
- **Bean sprouts**: Lightly blanched
- **Spinach**: Lightly blanched or fresh
- **Nori (seaweed)**: Sheets, cut into strips
- **Green onions**: Chopped, for garnish
- **Sesame seeds**: For garnish (optional)

Instructions

Broth Preparation:

1. **Prepare the Bones**: Rinse the chicken or pork bones under cold water. Place them in a large pot and cover with cold water. Bring to a boil over high heat. Once boiling, discard the water and rinse the bones. This step helps remove impurities.
2. **Simmer the Broth**: Return the bones to the pot and add fresh water to cover. Bring to a boil, then reduce the heat to low. Simmer for 2-3 hours, skimming off any foam or fat that rises to the surface.
3. **Add Aromatics**: Add the minced garlic, ginger, and green onions to the pot. Simmer for another 10 minutes.
4. **Strain the Broth**: Strain the broth through a fine-mesh sieve into another pot. Discard the solids.

5. **Season the Broth**: Stir in the miso paste until fully dissolved. Add soy sauce, mirin, and sake if using. Taste and adjust seasoning if needed.

Chashu Pork (Optional):

1. **Ingredients**: 500 grams (about 1 pound) pork belly, soy sauce, mirin, sake, sugar, and water.
2. **Prepare**: Roll the pork belly into a log and tie with kitchen twine.
3. **Cook**: Sear the pork in a hot pan until browned on all sides. Add soy sauce, mirin, sake, sugar, and enough water to cover the pork. Simmer for 2-3 hours or until tender. Slice thinly once cooled.

Soft-Boiled Eggs (Marinated):

1. **Ingredients**: 4 large eggs, soy sauce, mirin, and a little sugar.
2. **Cook**: Boil the eggs for 7 minutes for a slightly runny yolk or 8 minutes for a firmer yolk. Cool in ice water.
3. **Marinate**: Peel the eggs and marinate in a mixture of soy sauce, mirin, and a little sugar for at least 1 hour or overnight in the refrigerator.

Assembly:

1. **Prepare Noodles**: Cook the ramen noodles according to package instructions. Drain and divide among bowls.
2. **Add Broth**: Pour the hot miso broth over the noodles in each bowl.
3. **Top**: Add slices of chashu pork, halved marinated eggs, corn, bean sprouts, spinach, and nori strips. Garnish with chopped green onions and sesame seeds if desired.
4. **Serve**: Enjoy your Miso Ramen hot!

Tips

- **Miso Variety**: Red miso will give a stronger flavor, while white miso is milder and sweeter. Adjust based on your taste preference.
- **Broth Clarity**: Skimming off impurities and fat during simmering helps keep the broth clear and clean-tasting.
- **Noodles**: Fresh ramen noodles are ideal, but you can use dried noodles if that's what you have on hand.

Enjoy making and eating your rich and flavorful Miso Ramen!

Miso Soup with Mushrooms

Ingredients

For the Soup:

- **Dashi**: 4 cups (you can use instant dashi or make your own with kombu and bonito flakes)
- **Miso paste**: 3-4 tablespoons (white, red, or a blend)
- **Shiitake mushrooms**: 1 cup, sliced (fresh or rehydrated if using dried)
- **Tofu**: 1 block (silken or firm), cut into cubes
- **Green onions**: 2-3, chopped
- **Wakame seaweed**: 1/4 cup, dried (rehydrated if using dried)
- **Optional**: Enoki mushrooms or other mushrooms of your choice

Instructions

1. **Prepare the Dashi**:
    - **Instant Dashi**: Dissolve according to package instructions.
    - **Homemade Dashi**: Simmer kombu (dried kelp) in water, then add bonito flakes and strain.
2. **Prepare the Ingredients**:
    - **Mushrooms**: If using dried shiitake mushrooms, rehydrate them in warm water for about 20 minutes. Slice them once rehydrated.
    - **Wakame**: Soak dried wakame seaweed in water for 5 minutes, then drain and cut into bite-sized pieces if needed.
    - **Tofu**: Cut into cubes and set aside.
3. **Simmer the Soup**:
    - In a pot, bring the dashi to a simmer over medium heat.
    - Add the sliced mushrooms and cook for 5-7 minutes until they are tender and have released their flavor into the broth.
4. **Add Tofu and Wakame**:
    - Add the tofu cubes and wakame seaweed to the pot. Simmer gently for another 2-3 minutes, being careful not to boil vigorously to avoid breaking up the tofu.
5. **Incorporate Miso Paste**:
    - Place the miso paste in a small bowl or ladle. Scoop some of the hot broth into the bowl and stir to dissolve the miso paste into a smooth mixture.
    - Return the miso mixture to the pot. Stir gently and heat through, but do not boil, as boiling can affect the flavor and texture of the miso.
6. **Finish and Serve**:
    - Taste the soup and adjust seasoning if necessary. You can add more miso paste if you prefer a stronger flavor.
    - Garnish with chopped green onions before serving.

Tips

- **Miso Paste**: White miso is milder and sweeter, while red miso is stronger and saltier. You can mix them to balance the flavor according to your preference.
- **Avoid Boiling**: Once the miso paste is added, keep the soup at a simmer rather than a boil to maintain the delicate flavors and beneficial probiotics in miso.
- **Variety**: Feel free to add other vegetables like sliced carrots or greens if desired.

This Miso Soup with Mushrooms is perfect as a light meal or as a side dish to accompany a Japanese-style dinner. Enjoy the warm, savory flavors!

Kabocha Tempura (Pumpkin Tempura)

Ingredients

For the Tempura:

- **Kabocha squash**: 1 small to medium, peeled and cut into thin wedges or bite-sized pieces
- **All-purpose flour**: 1 cup
- **Cornstarch**: 1/4 cup
- **Baking powder**: 1 teaspoon
- **Cold water**: 1 cup (ice-cold for best results)
- **Egg**: 1 large (optional, for a richer batter)
- **Vegetable oil**: For frying (enough for deep frying)

For Serving:

- **Tempura dipping sauce (Tentsuyu)**: You can make it by mixing equal parts soy sauce, mirin, and dashi. Heat and let it cool before serving.

Instructions

1. **Prepare the Kabocha**:
   - Peel the kabocha squash if it's not pre-peeled. Cut it into thin wedges or bite-sized pieces. Remove the seeds if necessary.
   - **Tip**: To make slicing easier, you can microwave the kabocha for a few minutes to soften it slightly before cutting.
2. **Prepare the Batter**:
   - In a mixing bowl, combine flour, cornstarch, and baking powder.
   - In a separate bowl, lightly beat the egg (if using) and then add the ice-cold water.
   - Add the wet ingredients to the dry ingredients and mix briefly. The batter should be lumpy; don't overmix. The ice-cold water helps create a crispier texture.
3. **Heat the Oil**:
   - In a deep pan or fryer, heat enough vegetable oil to submerge the kabocha pieces to 350-375°F (175-190°C). Use a thermometer to check the temperature.
4. **Coat and Fry**:
   - Dip the kabocha pieces into the tempura batter, allowing excess batter to drip off.
   - Carefully slide the battered kabocha into the hot oil. Fry in batches, making sure not to overcrowd the pan. Fry until golden brown and crispy, about 3-4 minutes.
   - Use a slotted spoon to remove the tempura from the oil and drain on paper towels.
5. **Serve**:
   - Serve the kabocha tempura hot with tempura dipping sauce (tentsuyu) for dipping. You can also enjoy it with a sprinkle of sea salt if you prefer.

Tips

- **Batter Temperature**: Keep the batter cold by using ice-cold water and working quickly to ensure a crispy texture.
- **Oil Temperature**: Maintain a consistent oil temperature to avoid soggy or overly greasy tempura. Too hot and the batter will burn quickly; too cold and it will absorb excess oil.
- **Optional Add-ins**: You can also tempura other vegetables or seafood alongside the kabocha for a variety of flavors.

Kabocha Tempura is a great side dish, appetizer, or even a light main course. Enjoy the crispy, sweet, and savory treat!

Katsudon (Pork Cutlet Rice Bowl)

Ingredients

For the Tonkatsu (Pork Cutlet):

- **Pork loin or pork tenderloin**: 4 pieces, about 1/2 inch thick
- **Salt**: 1/2 teaspoon
- **Black pepper**: 1/4 teaspoon
- **Flour**: 1/2 cup
- **Egg**: 1, beaten
- **Panko breadcrumbs**: 1 cup
- **Vegetable oil**: For frying

For the Katsudon Sauce:

- **Onion**: 1 medium, thinly sliced
- **Eggs**: 2, lightly beaten
- **Dashi**: 1 cup (you can use instant dashi or homemade)
- **Soy sauce**: 2 tablespoons
- **Mirin**: 2 tablespoons
- **Sugar**: 1 tablespoon

For Serving:

- **Cooked rice**: 4 bowls, hot
- **Green onions**: Chopped, for garnish (optional)
- **Pickled ginger**: For garnish (optional)

Instructions

1. Prepare the Tonkatsu:

1. **Season the Pork**: Lightly season the pork cutlets with salt and pepper.
2. **Bread the Pork**: Dredge each cutlet in flour, shaking off excess. Dip in beaten egg, then coat with panko breadcrumbs, pressing gently to adhere.
3. **Fry the Cutlets**: Heat vegetable oil in a deep skillet or pan over medium heat. Fry the cutlets for 4-5 minutes on each side, or until golden brown and cooked through. Drain on paper towels and slice into strips.

2. Prepare the Katsudon Sauce:

1. **Cook the Onion**: In a skillet, add a little oil and cook the sliced onion until soft and translucent.
2. **Add the Sauce Ingredients**: Add the dashi, soy sauce, mirin, and sugar to the skillet. Stir to combine and bring to a simmer.

3. **Add the Pork**: Place the sliced pork cutlets into the skillet with the sauce. Allow them to simmer for a few minutes so they absorb the flavors.

3. Add the Eggs:

1. **Pour the Eggs**: Pour the beaten eggs evenly over the pork and onions. Cover the skillet and cook for about 1-2 minutes, or until the eggs are set but still slightly soft.

4. Assemble the Katsudon:

1. **Serve Over Rice**: Place a serving of hot cooked rice in each bowl.
2. **Top with Pork and Sauce**: Spoon the pork and sauce mixture over the rice.
3. **Garnish**: Top with chopped green onions and pickled ginger if desired.

Tips

- **Oil Temperature**: Ensure the oil is at the right temperature (around 350°F or 175°C) for crispy, golden-brown cutlets.
- **Egg Consistency**: For a traditional katsudon, the eggs should be slightly runny. Adjust the cooking time if you prefer them firmer.
- **Serving**: Katsudon is best enjoyed immediately while the cutlet is crispy and the rice is hot.

Enjoy your homemade Katsudon—a comforting and flavorful dish that's sure to satisfy!

Tori Dango (Chicken Meatballs)

Ingredients

For the Meatballs:

- **Ground chicken**: 500 grams (about 1 pound)
- **Green onion**: 2-3 stalks, finely chopped
- **Ginger**: 1-inch piece, grated
- **Garlic**: 2 cloves, minced
- **Soy sauce**: 2 tablespoons
- **Mirin**: 1 tablespoon
- **Sesame oil**: 1 tablespoon
- **Salt**: 1/2 teaspoon
- **Black pepper**: 1/4 teaspoon
- **Panko breadcrumbs**: 1/4 cup (for binding and texture)
- **Egg**: 1 (optional, for binding)

For the Glaze (optional but recommended):

- **Soy sauce**: 1/4 cup
- **Mirin**: 2 tablespoons
- **Sugar**: 1 tablespoon
- **Water**: 2 tablespoons

For Garnish:

- **Chopped green onions**: For garnish
- **Sesame seeds**: For garnish (optional)

Instructions

1. Prepare the Meatball Mixture:

1. In a large bowl, combine ground chicken, finely chopped green onion, grated ginger, minced garlic, soy sauce, mirin, sesame oil, salt, and black pepper.
2. Add the panko breadcrumbs and mix well. If the mixture feels too loose, you can add an egg to help bind it together.

2. Form the Meatballs:

1. Wet your hands to prevent sticking and shape the mixture into small meatballs, about 1 to 1.5 inches in diameter. You should get about 20-25 meatballs depending on size.

3. Cook the Meatballs:

- **Pan-Frying**: Heat a little oil in a non-stick skillet over medium heat. Add the meatballs and cook, turning occasionally, until they are golden brown and cooked through, about 10-12 minutes.
- **Baking**: Preheat the oven to 375°F (190°C). Place the meatballs on a baking sheet lined with parchment paper and bake for 20-25 minutes, or until fully cooked and golden brown.

4. Prepare the Glaze (Optional):

1. In a small saucepan, combine soy sauce, mirin, sugar, and water. Bring to a simmer over medium heat and cook until the sauce is slightly thickened, about 5 minutes.

5. Glaze the Meatballs (Optional):

1. If using the glaze, brush or drizzle it over the cooked meatballs, or toss them in the glaze in a bowl.

6. Serve:

1. Transfer the meatballs to a serving dish.
2. Garnish with chopped green onions and sesame seeds if desired.

Tips

- **Texture**: If the meatball mixture is too wet, add a bit more panko breadcrumbs. If it's too dry, a small amount of water or another egg can help.
- **Flavor Variations**: You can add finely chopped vegetables, like bell peppers or mushrooms, to the mixture for added flavor and texture.
- **Storage**: Leftover meatballs can be stored in the refrigerator for up to 3 days or frozen for up to 2 months.

Enjoy your Tori Dango as a tasty and versatile dish that's perfect for any occasion!

Shio Ramen (Salt Ramen)

Ingredients

For the Broth:

- **Chicken or pork bones**: 500 grams (about 1 pound), preferably with some meat on them
- **Water**: Enough to cover the bones
- **Dashi**: 4 cups (optional, for extra depth of flavor; can use instant dashi or homemade)
- **Salt**: To taste
- **Soy sauce**: 1-2 tablespoons (optional, for a bit of color and added umami)
- **Ginger**: 1-inch piece, sliced
- **Garlic**: 2-3 cloves, smashed
- **Green onions**: 2-3, cut into large pieces

For the Toppings:

- **Ramen noodles**: 4 servings, cooked according to package instructions
- **Chashu pork**: Slices (recipe below) or store-bought
- **Soft-boiled eggs**: 4, marinated (recipe below)
- **Green onions**: Chopped
- **Bamboo shoots**: Sliced, pickled (optional)
- **Nori (seaweed)**: Sheets, cut into strips
- **Bean sprouts**: Lightly blanched (optional)
- **Corn**: Fresh or frozen (optional)
- **Spinach or other greens**: Lightly blanched or fresh

Instructions

Broth Preparation:

1. **Prepare the Bones**: Rinse the chicken or pork bones under cold water. Place them in a large pot and cover with cold water. Bring to a boil over high heat. Once boiling, discard the water and rinse the bones. This step helps remove impurities and results in a clearer broth.
2. **Simmer the Broth**: Return the bones to the pot and add fresh water to cover. Bring to a boil, then reduce the heat to low. Simmer for 2-3 hours, skimming off any foam or fat that rises to the surface.
3. **Add Aromatics**: Add ginger, garlic, and green onions to the pot. Continue to simmer for another 10-15 minutes to infuse the broth with flavor.
4. **Strain the Broth**: Strain the broth through a fine-mesh sieve into another pot. Discard the solids.
5. **Season the Broth**: Stir in salt to taste. You can also add a small amount of soy sauce if you prefer a slightly richer flavor.

Chashu Pork (Optional):

1. **Ingredients**: 500 grams (about 1 pound) pork belly, soy sauce, mirin, sake, sugar, and water.
2. **Prepare**: Roll the pork belly into a log and tie with kitchen twine.
3. **Cook**: Sear the pork in a hot pan until browned on all sides. Add soy sauce, mirin, sake, sugar, and enough water to cover the pork. Simmer for 2-3 hours or until tender. Slice thinly once cooled.

Soft-Boiled Eggs (Marinated):

1. **Ingredients**: 4 large eggs, soy sauce, mirin, and a little sugar.
2. **Cook**: Boil the eggs for 7 minutes for a slightly runny yolk or 8 minutes for a firmer yolk. Cool in ice water.
3. **Marinate**: Peel the eggs and marinate in a mixture of soy sauce, mirin, and a little sugar for at least 1 hour or overnight in the refrigerator.

Assembly:

1. **Prepare Noodles**: Cook the ramen noodles according to package instructions. Drain and divide among bowls.
2. **Add Broth**: Pour the hot salt broth over the noodles in each bowl.
3. **Top**: Add slices of chashu pork, halved marinated eggs, and any additional toppings you like such as bamboo shoots, bean sprouts, corn, and greens. Garnish with chopped green onions and nori strips.
4. **Serve**: Enjoy your Shio Ramen hot!

Tips

- **Broth Clarity**: Skimming off impurities during simmering helps keep the broth clear and clean-tasting.
- **Noodles**: Fresh ramen noodles are ideal, but you can use dried noodles if that's what you have on hand.
- **Customizing**: Feel free to add other toppings or adjust the seasoning to suit your taste.

Shio Ramen offers a light yet deeply satisfying flavor, making it a perfect choice for those who appreciate the simplicity and elegance of Japanese cuisine. Enjoy your homemade bowl of Shio Ramen!

Nabeyaki Udon (Hot Pot Udon)

Ingredients

For the Broth:

- **Dashi**: 4 cups (you can use instant dashi or homemade with kombu and bonito flakes)
- **Soy sauce**: 2 tablespoons
- **Mirin**: 2 tablespoons
- **Sake**: 2 tablespoons (optional)
- **Sugar**: 1 teaspoon (optional, to balance the flavor)

For the Hot Pot:

- **Udon noodles**: 4 servings (fresh or frozen; if using dried, cook according to package instructions before adding to the hot pot)
- **Chicken**: 200 grams (about 7 ounces), thinly sliced (boneless thigh or breast)
- **Shiitaake mushrooms**: 4-6, sliced (or other mushrooms like enoki or maitake)
- **Japanese fish cake (kamaboko)**: 1/2 cup, sliced (or use any fish cakes you like)
- **Green onions**: 2-3, chopped
- **Carrots**: 1 medium, sliced
- **Spinach or bok choy**: A handful, blanched or fresh
- **Eggs**: 4, one per serving (optional, for poaching in the hot pot)
- **Napa cabbage or other leafy greens**: A few leaves, chopped (optional)

For Garnish (optional):

- **Tempura**: Shrimp or vegetable tempura (pre-cooked, for adding a crispy texture)
- **Shichimi togarashi**: A Japanese spice blend (for a bit of heat)
- **Sesame seeds**: For garnish
- **Chopped fresh parsley or cilantro**: For garnish

Instructions

1. Prepare the Broth:

- In a large pot, combine the dashi, soy sauce, mirin, sake (if using), and sugar (if using). Bring to a gentle simmer.

2. Prepare the Ingredients:

- **Udon Noodles**: If using dried noodles, cook them according to package instructions, then drain and set aside.
- **Vegetables**: Slice the shiitake mushrooms, carrots, and fish cake. Prepare your greens (spinach, bok choy, or napa cabbage).
- **Chicken**: Slice the chicken into thin pieces.

3. Assemble the Hot Pot:

- Add the sliced chicken, mushrooms, fish cake, carrots, and any other vegetables to the simmering broth. Cook for about 5-7 minutes, until the chicken is cooked through and the vegetables are tender.
- Add the cooked udon noodles to the pot and gently stir to combine. Simmer for an additional 2-3 minutes to heat the noodles through.

4. Poach the Eggs (Optional):

- If using eggs, gently crack them into the hot pot, making sure they don't break. Allow them to poach in the simmering broth until the whites are set but the yolks are still runny, about 2-3 minutes. You can cover the pot to help the eggs cook evenly.

5. Serve:

- Ladle the udon, broth, and toppings into individual bowls.
- Garnish with chopped green onions, sesame seeds, and shichimi togarashi if desired.
- Add tempura on the side or on top if using.

Tips

- **Flavor Adjustments**: Taste the broth and adjust the seasoning with more soy sauce or mirin if needed. The broth should be savory but not overly salty.
- **Noodle Preparation**: If preparing ahead, keep the udon noodles separate from the broth and add them just before serving to prevent them from becoming overly soft.
- **Toppings**: Feel free to customize your hot pot with other vegetables or proteins like tofu, seafood, or additional mushrooms.

Nabeyaki Udon is a versatile and hearty dish that's perfect for warming up on a cold day or enjoying with friends and family. Enjoy your homemade hot pot!

Kakiage (Mixed Vegetable Tempura)

Ingredients

For the Kakiage:

- **Carrots**: 1 medium, julienned
- **Onion**: 1 large, thinly sliced
- **Sweet potato**: 1 small, julienned (optional)
- **Green beans or bell pepper**: 1/2 cup, thinly sliced (optional)
- **Shiitake mushrooms**: 4-5, thinly sliced (optional)
- **All-purpose flour**: 1/2 cup
- **Cornstarch**: 1/4 cup
- **Baking powder**: 1/2 teaspoon
- **Cold water**: 1/2 cup (ice-cold for the best texture)
- **Egg**: 1 large
- **Salt**: 1/2 teaspoon
- **Black pepper**: 1/4 teaspoon

For Frying:

- **Vegetable oil**: For deep frying

For Serving:

- **Tempura dipping sauce (Tentsuyu)**: You can make it by mixing equal parts soy sauce, mirin, and dashi. Heat and let it cool before serving.

Instructions

1. Prepare the Vegetables:

- Julienne the carrots, sweet potato, and any other vegetables you're using.
- Thinly slice the onion and other optional vegetables like bell pepper and mushrooms.

2. Prepare the Batter:

1. In a large bowl, combine the all-purpose flour, cornstarch, baking powder, salt, and black pepper.
2. In another bowl, lightly beat the egg and then add the ice-cold water.
3. Add the wet ingredients to the dry ingredients and mix until just combined. The batter should be lumpy and thick.

3. Mix the Vegetables:

- Gently fold the vegetables into the batter, making sure they are well-coated but not overly mixed.

4. Heat the Oil:

- Heat vegetable oil in a deep pan or fryer to 350°F (175°C). Use enough oil to submerge the kakiage.

5. Fry the Kakiage:

- Drop spoonfuls of the batter mixture into the hot oil, forming small mounds or patties. You can use two spoons or a small ice cream scoop to help with this.
- Fry in batches to avoid overcrowding. Cook each batch for about 3-4 minutes, or until golden brown and crispy, turning occasionally to ensure even cooking.
- Use a slotted spoon to remove the kakiage from the oil and drain on paper towels.

6. Serve:

- Serve the kakiage hot with tempura dipping sauce (tentsuyu) on the side. You can also enjoy it with a sprinkle of sea salt.

Tips

- **Batter Temperature**: Using ice-cold water helps create a crispier texture in the batter.
- **Oil Temperature**: Maintaining the oil at the right temperature ensures that the kakiage is crispy and not greasy. If the oil is too cool, the kakiage will absorb more oil and become soggy.
- **Vegetable Variations**: Feel free to adjust the vegetable mix based on what you have available or to suit your taste preferences.

Kakiage is a delicious way to enjoy a variety of vegetables with a crispy and light batter. It's perfect as an appetizer, side dish, or even as a topping for rice or noodles. Enjoy!

Miso Yaki Onigiri (Grilled Rice Balls)

Ingredients

For the Rice Balls:

- **Japanese short-grain rice**: 2 cups
- **Water**: 2 1/2 cups (for cooking the rice)
- **Salt**: To taste

For the Miso Glaze:

- **Miso paste**: 3 tablespoons (white miso or a mix of white and red miso)
- **Mirin**: 2 tablespoons
- **Soy sauce**: 1 tablespoon
- **Sugar**: 1 tablespoon
- **Sake**: 1 tablespoon (optional)

Instructions

1. Cook the Rice:

- Rinse the rice under cold water until the water runs clear to remove excess starch.
- Combine the rinsed rice and water in a rice cooker or pot. Cook according to your rice cooker's instructions or bring to a boil, then reduce heat to low, cover, and simmer for 15-20 minutes until the water is absorbed and the rice is tender.
- Let the rice sit covered for about 10 minutes after cooking to allow it to firm up slightly.

2. Prepare the Miso Glaze:

- In a small saucepan, combine the miso paste, mirin, soy sauce, sugar, and sake (if using). Cook over medium heat, stirring constantly, until the mixture is smooth and slightly thickened. Remove from heat and let it cool.

3. Form the Rice Balls:

- Wet your hands with water to prevent the rice from sticking. Take a portion of rice (about 1/4 cup) and shape it into a triangle or oval, pressing gently to form a compact ball. Repeat with the remaining rice.

4. Grill the Rice Balls:

- Preheat a grill or grill pan over medium heat. Lightly oil the grill grates or pan to prevent sticking.
- Place the rice balls on the grill and cook for about 2-3 minutes on each side, or until they are golden brown and crispy. You can also use a broiler if you don't have a grill.

5. Apply the Miso Glaze:

- Brush the miso glaze onto the grilled rice balls, then return them to the grill for an additional 1-2 minutes per side, allowing the glaze to caramelize and become slightly sticky. Be careful not to let it burn.

6. Serve:

- Serve the miso yaki onigiri warm, garnished with additional toppings if desired (like sesame seeds or chopped green onions).

Tips

- **Rice Preparation**: Using short-grain or medium-grain Japanese rice is essential for achieving the right texture. If using sushi rice, follow the same steps.
- **Miso Glaze**: Adjust the sweetness and saltiness of the glaze to your taste. You can also experiment with different types of miso paste for varied flavors.
- **Grilling**: Watch the rice balls closely while grilling to avoid burning. The glaze can caramelize quickly.

Miso Yaki Onigiri are perfect for a quick snack, a side dish, or even a fun addition to a bento box. Enjoy the savory, smoky flavors and crispy texture of these delicious grilled rice balls!

Tori Kotsu Ramen (Chicken Bone Broth Ramen)

Ingredients

For the Broth:

- **Chicken bones**: 2-3 pounds (wings, backs, and/or carcasses)
- **Water**: Enough to cover the bones (about 6-8 cups)
- **Ginger**: 1 large piece, sliced
- **Garlic**: 4-5 cloves, smashed
- **Green onions**: 2-3, cut into large pieces
- **Onion**: 1 large, cut into chunks
- **Carrots**: 1-2, cut into chunks (optional)
- **Soy sauce**: 2-3 tablespoons (for seasoning)
- **Salt**: To taste

For the Toppings:

- **Ramen noodles**: 4 servings (fresh or dried)
- **Chicken**: 1-2 chicken thighs or breasts, cooked and sliced (you can use leftover or poached chicken)
- **Soft-boiled eggs**: 4 (marinated in soy sauce and mirin, optional)
- **Bamboo shoots**: 1/2 cup, sliced (optional)
- **Green onions**: Chopped
- **Nori (seaweed)**: Sheets, cut into strips
- **Corn**: Fresh or frozen (optional)
- **Spinach or bok choy**: Lightly blanched (optional)
- **Menma (fermented bamboo shoots)**: Optional

For the Seasoning (Optional):

- **Miso paste**: 1-2 tablespoons (for added umami)
- **Sesame oil**: 1 teaspoon (for added richness)

Instructions

1. Prepare the Broth:

1. **Blanch the Bones**: Rinse the chicken bones under cold water. Place them in a large pot and cover with cold water. Bring to a boil, then discard the water and rinse the bones to remove impurities.
2. **Simmer the Broth**: Return the cleaned bones to the pot and cover with fresh water. Add the ginger, garlic, green onions, onion, and carrots (if using). Bring to a boil, then reduce heat to low and simmer for 3-4 hours. Skim off any foam or impurities that rise to the surface.

3. **Strain the Broth**: Strain the broth through a fine-mesh sieve into another pot. Discard the solids.

2. Season the Broth:

1. **Add Seasoning**: Season the broth with soy sauce and salt to taste. You can also stir in miso paste for added depth of flavor if desired.
2. **Optional**: For a richer flavor, add a small amount of sesame oil to the broth.

3. Prepare the Toppings:

1. **Cook the Chicken**: If not using pre-cooked chicken, you can poach or grill the chicken thighs or breasts. Season with salt and pepper, cook until done, and then slice thinly.
2. **Marinate the Eggs**: If marinating, mix equal parts soy sauce and mirin and soak the boiled eggs for at least an hour or overnight for more flavor.

4. Cook the Noodles:

- Cook the ramen noodles according to the package instructions. Drain and rinse under cold water to stop cooking.

5. Assemble the Ramen:

1. **Reheat Broth**: Bring the broth back to a simmer.
2. **Prepare Bowls**: Divide the cooked noodles among serving bowls.
3. **Add Toppings**: Top with sliced chicken, soft-boiled eggs, bamboo shoots, green onions, nori strips, corn, spinach or bok choy, and menma if using.
4. **Pour Broth**: Ladle the hot broth over the noodles and toppings in each bowl.

Tips

- **Broth Clarity**: Blanching the bones before simmering helps keep the broth clear.
- **Richness**: For a creamier texture, you can blend some of the broth with a little of the cooked chicken meat and then return it to the pot.
- **Noodle Choice**: Fresh ramen noodles will give you the best texture, but dried noodles work well too.

Enjoy your Tori Kotsu Ramen, with its rich, flavorful broth and satisfying toppings. It's a comforting bowl of goodness perfect for any time of year!

Kimchi Nabe (Kimchi Hot Pot)

Ingredients

For the Broth:

- **Kimchi**: 1-2 cups (with some of its juice; adjust based on how spicy and tangy you want the broth)
- **Chicken or vegetable broth**: 4 cups (you can use store-bought or homemade)
- **Soy sauce**: 2 tablespoons
- **Mirin**: 2 tablespoons
- **Sake**: 2 tablespoons (optional)
- **Garlic**: 3 cloves, minced
- **Ginger**: 1-inch piece, sliced
- **Green onions**: 2-3 stalks, cut into large pieces
- **Sesame oil**: 1 tablespoon

For the Hot Pot:

- **Tofu**: 1 block, cut into cubes (firm or silken, based on preference)
- **Shiitake mushrooms**: 4-5, sliced (or other mushrooms like enoki or oyster mushrooms)
- **Carrots**: 1 medium, thinly sliced
- **Daikon radish**: 1/2 medium, thinly sliced (optional)
- **Napa cabbage or bok choy**: A few leaves, chopped
- **Green onions**: Chopped, for garnish
- **Bean sprouts**: 1 cup (optional)
- **Sliced pork or chicken**: 200 grams (about 7 ounces), thinly sliced (optional)
- **Rice cakes (tteokbokki)**: 1 cup (optional)

For Serving:

- **Cooked rice**: Steamed white rice or short-grain rice
- **Chopped cilantro or parsley**: For garnish (optional)

Instructions

1. Prepare the Broth:

1. In a large pot, heat the sesame oil over medium heat. Add the minced garlic and sliced ginger, and cook until fragrant, about 1-2 minutes.
2. Add the kimchi and its juice to the pot and cook for another 2-3 minutes, stirring occasionally.
3. Pour in the chicken or vegetable broth, soy sauce, mirin, and sake (if using). Bring to a simmer and let it cook for about 10-15 minutes to allow the flavors to meld.

2. Prepare the Ingredients:

- **Tofu**: Cut into cubes.
- **Vegetables**: Slice the mushrooms, carrots, and daikon radish. Chop the napa cabbage or bok choy.
- **Meat (Optional)**: Slice the pork or chicken thinly if using.
- **Rice Cakes (Optional)**: If using, soak them in water if they're dried.

3. Add Ingredients to the Pot:

1. Add the tofu cubes, mushrooms, carrots, daikon radish, and sliced meat (if using) to the simmering broth. Cook for about 5-7 minutes, or until the meat and vegetables are tender.
2. Add the napa cabbage or bok choy and bean sprouts (if using) and cook for an additional 2-3 minutes, until the greens are wilted.
3. Add the rice cakes (if using) and cook for another 2-3 minutes until they are heated through.

4. Serve:

- Ladle the hot pot ingredients and broth into individual bowls.
- Serve with steamed rice on the side.
- Garnish with chopped green onions and cilantro or parsley if desired.

Tips

- **Kimchi**: Use well-fermented kimchi for a richer, deeper flavor. Adjust the amount of kimchi and its juice based on how spicy and tangy you like the broth.
- **Vegetable and Meat Variations**: Feel free to add or substitute other vegetables and proteins based on your preferences.
- **Rice Cakes**: If you can't find Korean rice cakes, you can substitute with regular rice noodles or omit them.

Kimchi Nabe is a versatile and comforting dish that combines the spicy tang of kimchi with a variety of fresh ingredients, making it perfect for a cozy meal. Enjoy!

Udon in Broth

Ingredients

For the Broth:

- **Dashi**: 4 cups (homemade with kombu and bonito flakes or instant dashi powder)
- **Soy sauce**: 2-3 tablespoons (to taste)
- **Mirin**: 2 tablespoons
- **Sake**: 2 tablespoons (optional)
- **Salt**: To taste
- **Sugar**: 1 teaspoon (optional, for balance)

For the Udon:

- **Udon noodles**: 4 servings (fresh or frozen; if using dried, cook according to package instructions before adding to the broth)
- **Green onions**: 2-3 stalks, chopped
- **Shiitake mushrooms**: 4-5, sliced (or other mushrooms like enoki or maitake)
- **Tofu**: 1 block, cubed (firm or silken, based on preference)
- **Spinach or bok choy**: A handful, blanched (optional)
- **Carrots**: 1 medium, thinly sliced (optional)
- **Napa cabbage**: A few leaves, chopped (optional)
- **Kamaboko (fish cake)**: 1/2 cup, sliced (optional)
- **Seaweed (nori or wakame)**: Cut into strips (optional)
- **Soft-boiled egg**: 1-2 per serving (marinated if desired)

Instructions

1. Prepare the Broth:

1. **Make Dashi**: If using homemade dashi, soak a piece of kombu (dried kelp) in water for about 30 minutes, then heat the water until just before boiling. Remove the kombu and add bonito flakes. Simmer for a few minutes, then strain. If using instant dashi powder, dissolve it in water according to package instructions.
2. **Season the Broth**: In a pot, combine the dashi with soy sauce, mirin, and sake (if using). Adjust the seasoning with salt and sugar to taste. Heat the mixture to a simmer.

2. Prepare the Udon and Toppings:

- **Cook the Udon**: If using dried udon, cook according to the package instructions. Drain and set aside. If using fresh or frozen udon, just thaw or briefly heat them before adding to the broth.
- **Prepare Toppings**: Slice mushrooms, cube tofu, and prepare any other vegetables or toppings. Blanch or cook vegetables like spinach, bok choy, or carrots if needed.

3. Combine Ingredients:

1. **Add Toppings**: Add the sliced mushrooms, tofu, and any other vegetables or fish cakes to the simmering broth. Cook for about 5-7 minutes until the vegetables are tender and the tofu is heated through.
2. **Add Udon**: Add the cooked udon noodles to the pot and simmer for an additional 2-3 minutes, or until the noodles are heated through and have absorbed some of the broth flavor.

4. Serve:

- Divide the noodles and broth among serving bowls.
- Garnish with chopped green onions, seaweed, and a soft-boiled egg if desired.

Tips

- **Broth Depth**: Adjust the broth seasoning to your taste. Adding a small amount of sugar can help balance the flavors, especially if the broth is too salty or tangy.
- **Noodle Texture**: For the best texture, ensure that the udon noodles are cooked just before adding them to the broth so they retain their chewiness.
- **Toppings**: Customize your udon with a variety of toppings based on what you have available or your personal preferences.

Udon in Broth is a versatile and comforting dish that can be enjoyed year-round. It's perfect for a quick meal or a more elaborate dinner with a variety of toppings. Enjoy your bowl of delicious, homemade udon!

Mochi Soup with Vegetables

Ingredients

For the Broth:

- **Dashi**: 4 cups (homemade with kombu and bonito flakes or instant dashi powder)
- **Soy sauce**: 2 tablespoons
- **Mirin**: 2 tablespoons
- **Salt**: To taste
- **Sugar**: 1 teaspoon (optional, to balance flavors)

For the Soup:

- **Mochi rice cakes**: 4-6 pieces (preferably the round or square type; if using frozen, thaw them before cooking)
- **Carrots**: 1 medium, sliced thinly
- **Daikon radish**: 1/2 medium, sliced thinly
- **Napa cabbage or bok choy**: A few leaves, chopped
- **Shiitake mushrooms**: 4-5, sliced (or other mushrooms like enoki or maitake)
- **Green onions**: 2-3 stalks, chopped
- **Spinach**: A handful (optional)
- **Tofu**: 1 block, cubed (optional, for extra protein)

Instructions

1. Prepare the Broth:

1. **Make Dashi**: If using homemade dashi, soak a piece of kombu (dried kelp) in water for about 30 minutes, then heat the water until just before boiling. Remove the kombu and add bonito flakes. Simmer for a few minutes, then strain. If using instant dashi powder, dissolve it in water according to package instructions.
2. **Season the Broth**: In a pot, combine the dashi with soy sauce, mirin, and salt. Taste and adjust seasoning with sugar if needed. Bring to a simmer.

2. Prepare the Vegetables:

- Slice the carrots and daikon radish thinly.
- Chop the napa cabbage or bok choy and slice the mushrooms.
- Cube the tofu if using.

3. Cook the Vegetables:

- In a separate pot, add the sliced carrots, daikon radish, and mushrooms to the simmering broth. Cook for about 5-7 minutes until the vegetables are tender.

- Add the napa cabbage or bok choy and cook for another 2-3 minutes until wilted. Add spinach if using and cook for another minute.

4. Prepare the Mochi:

- **If Fresh**: Grill or pan-fry the mochi pieces until they are golden and slightly crispy on the outside.
- **If Frozen**: Thaw and grill or pan-fry as described above.

5. Combine and Serve:

- Add the mochi pieces to the pot with the vegetables and broth. Simmer for an additional 2-3 minutes until the mochi is heated through and slightly soft.
- Garnish with chopped green onions before serving.

Tips

- **Mochi Preparation**: Grilling or pan-frying the mochi before adding it to the soup gives it a nice texture and helps it absorb the broth flavors better.
- **Vegetable Variations**: Feel free to add other vegetables like celery, bell peppers, or mushrooms based on what you have on hand.
- **Broth Flavor**: Adjust the broth seasoning according to your taste. Adding a small amount of sugar can enhance the overall flavor of the soup.

Mochi Soup with Vegetables is a versatile and comforting dish that is great for any season. It combines the chewy texture of mochi with the savory flavors of the broth and fresh vegetables. Enjoy your homemade mochi soup!

Mizutaki (Chicken Hot Pot)

Ingredients

For the Broth:

- **Chicken**: 2-3 pounds (such as bone-in chicken thighs or drumsticks)
- **Water**: 8 cups
- **Ginger**: 1 large piece, sliced
- **Garlic**: 4-5 cloves, smashed
- **Green onions**: 2-3 stalks, cut into large pieces
- **Salt**: To taste

For the Hot Pot:

- **Tofu**: 1 block, cut into cubes (firm or silken, based on preference)
- **Shiitake mushrooms**: 4-5, sliced (or other mushrooms like enoki or maitake)
- **Carrots**: 2 medium, sliced thinly
- **Daikon radish**: 1/2 medium, sliced thinly
- **Napa cabbage or bok choy**: A few leaves, chopped
- **Spinach**: A handful (optional)
- **Green onions**: Chopped, for garnish
- **Mizuna or other leafy greens**: A handful (optional)

For Dipping Sauce:

- **Ponzu sauce**: 1/2 cup
- **Soy sauce**: 1 tablespoon (optional)
- **Grated daikon radish**: 1/2 cup (optional, for added flavor and texture)
- **Chopped green onions**: For garnish

Instructions

1. Prepare the Broth:

1. **Make the Stock**: Place the chicken pieces in a large pot and cover with water. Bring to a boil over high heat. Reduce heat and simmer for 5-10 minutes, skimming off any foam or impurities that rise to the surface.
2. **Add Aromatics**: Add the ginger, garlic, and green onions to the pot. Continue to simmer for 1-2 hours, partially covered, until the chicken is tender and the flavors are well developed. Add water as needed to keep the chicken covered.
3. **Strain the Broth**: Remove the chicken pieces and strain the broth through a fine-mesh sieve into a clean pot. Season with salt to taste.

2. Prepare the Ingredients:

- **Tofu**: Cut into bite-sized cubes.
- **Vegetables**: Slice the carrots and daikon radish thinly. Chop the napa cabbage or bok choy into pieces. Slice the mushrooms.
- **Garnishes**: Prepare chopped green onions and mizuna or other leafy greens if using.

3. Cook the Hot Pot:

1. **Heat the Broth**: Return the strained broth to the pot and bring it to a simmer.
2. **Add Ingredients**: Add the tofu cubes, carrots, daikon radish, mushrooms, and any other vegetables to the simmering broth. Cook for about 5-7 minutes, or until the vegetables are tender and the tofu is heated through.
3. **Add Leafy Greens**: Add the napa cabbage, bok choy, spinach, or mizuna and cook for another 1-2 minutes until the greens are wilted.

4. Serve:

- Ladle the hot pot ingredients and broth into individual bowls.
- Serve with dipping sauce on the side. You can use ponzu sauce as a tangy and savory dipping sauce, or mix it with soy sauce and grated daikon radish for added flavor.

Tips

- **Chicken Choice**: Using bone-in chicken parts adds more depth of flavor to the broth. You can also use chicken wings or backs for a more concentrated stock.
- **Broth Clarity**: Skimming off the foam during the initial boiling helps keep the broth clear.
- **Vegetable Variations**: Feel free to customize the vegetables based on seasonal availability or personal preference.
- **Dipping Sauce**: Adjust the dipping sauce to your taste. Ponzu sauce is a classic choice, but you can also serve the hot pot with a variety of sauces.

Mizutaki is a versatile and comforting hot pot dish that highlights the flavors of the broth and the freshness of the ingredients. It's perfect for a cozy meal and can be enjoyed year-round. Enjoy your Mizutaki!

Miso-Glazed Eggplant

Ingredients

For the Miso Glaze:

- **Miso paste**: 3 tablespoons (white miso is typically used, but red miso can also be used for a stronger flavor)
- **Mirin**: 2 tablespoons
- **Soy sauce**: 1 tablespoon
- **Sugar**: 1 tablespoon
- **Sesame oil**: 1 teaspoon
- **Water**: 1-2 tablespoons (to adjust the consistency)

For the Eggplant:

- **Eggplants**: 2 medium (Japanese eggplants or regular globe eggplants work well)
- **Salt**: To sprinkle on the eggplant
- **Oil**: For brushing or drizzling (vegetable oil or sesame oil works well)

Garnishes (Optional):

- **Sesame seeds**: Toasted
- **Chopped green onions**: For garnish
- **Chopped cilantro**: For garnish

Instructions

1. Prepare the Miso Glaze:

1. In a small bowl, whisk together the miso paste, mirin, soy sauce, sugar, and sesame oil until smooth.
2. Add water a little at a time to achieve a glaze consistency that's thick but spreadable. Set aside.

2. Prepare the Eggplant:

1. **Slice the Eggplant**: Cut the eggplants into 1/2-inch thick rounds or lengthwise slices, depending on your preference.
2. **Salt the Eggplant**: Sprinkle the eggplant slices with salt and let them sit for about 15-20 minutes. This helps draw out excess moisture and can reduce bitterness. After 15-20 minutes, rinse off the salt and pat the slices dry with paper towels.

3. Cook the Eggplant:

1. **Preheat the Oven**: If roasting, preheat the oven to 400°F (200°C). If using a grill, preheat it to medium-high heat.
2. **Oil the Eggplant**: Brush both sides of the eggplant slices with a small amount of oil.
3. **Cook the Eggplant**:
   - **Oven Method**: Arrange the eggplant slices on a baking sheet lined with parchment paper. Roast for about 20-25 minutes, flipping halfway through, until the eggplant is tender and golden brown.
   - **Grill Method**: Place the eggplant slices on the grill and cook for about 4-5 minutes per side, until tender and grill marks appear.

4. Apply the Miso Glaze:

1. **Glaze the Eggplant**: Once the eggplant is cooked, remove it from the oven or grill. Brush or spread the miso glaze evenly over the eggplant slices.
2. **Broil or Finish Cooking**: If using an oven, you can place the glazed eggplant slices under the broiler for 2-3 minutes to caramelize the glaze slightly. Watch closely to prevent burning.

5. Serve:

- Arrange the miso-glazed eggplant slices on a serving platter.
- Garnish with toasted sesame seeds, chopped green onions, and cilantro if desired.

Tips

- **Miso Paste**: Adjust the type and amount of miso paste based on your taste preference. White miso is milder and sweeter, while red miso is stronger and more savory.
- **Oil**: Using sesame oil to brush or drizzle on the eggplant adds extra flavor, but vegetable oil works well too.
- **Consistency**: If the miso glaze is too thick, add a little more water to thin it out.

Miso-Glazed Eggplant is a versatile dish that can be served as a side with rice or as part of a larger meal. Its combination of savory, sweet, and umami flavors makes it a hit with both family and friends. Enjoy!

www.ingramcontent.com/pod-product-compliance
Lightning Source LLC
LaVergne TN
LVHW081600060526
838201LV00054B/1996